Studies in Empirical Economics

Aman Ullah (Ed.)
Semiparametric and
Nonparametric Econometrics
1989. VII, 172 pp. Hard cover DM 120,—
ISBN 3-7908-0418-5

Walter Krämer (Ed.)
Econometrics of Structural Change
1989. X, 128 pp. Hard cover DM 85,—
ISBN 3-7908-0432-0

Wolfgang Franz (Ed.)

Hysteresis Effects in Economic Models

With 9 Figures

Physica-Verlag Heidelberg

Editor

Professor Dr. Wolfgang Franz
University of Konstanz
Economic Department
P.O.Box 5560
7750 Konstanz, FRG

First published in "Empirical Economics"
Vol. 15, No. 2, 1990

ISBN 3-7908-0482-7 Physica-Verlag Heidelberg
ISBN 0-387-91386-6 Springer-Verlag New York

CIP-Titelaufnahme der Deutschen Bibliothek

Hysteresis effects in economic models / Wolfgang Franz (Ed.).
– Heidelberg : Physica-Verl. ; New York : Springer, 1990
(Studies in empirical economics)
Aus: Empirical economics ; Vol. 15. 1990
ISBN 3-7908-0482-7 (Physica-Verl.) Gb.
ISBN 0-387-91386-6 (Springer) Gb.
NE: Franz, Wolfgang [Hrsg.]

Printed in Germany

Printing: Kiliandruck, Grünstadt
Bookbinding: T. Gansert GmbH, Weinheim-Sulzbach
7100/7130-543210

Preface

This volume is devoted to the hysteresis phenomenon in economic relationships. This topic has received renewed attention in economics especially in the late eighties. Since the issue is not settled there is still a growing literature on it. The aim of this volume is to summarize the findings, present new results, and to draw attention to further research.

All papers are written for this volume and are not published elsewhere. I am very grateful to all authors and referees without whose prompt and generous help this volume would not appear in the present form.

A short summary of each paper is given in section 5 of the overview paper.

Konstanz, January 1990

Wolfgang Franz
University of Konstanz

Contents

Hysteresis in Economic Relationships: An Overview

By W. Franz[1]

Can the socialist man be created
so as not to show any hysteresis trace
of his bourgois or peasant past?

N. Georgescu-Roegen (1971, p. 126)

1 Introduction

The hysteresis phenomenon has received renewed attention in economic science. While most of the theoretical work on hysteresis has been done within the context of an explanation of the persistence of European unemployment, there are other studies which investigate to what extent hysteresis is present in international trade, consumption, labor migration and the like. As it is often the case with "new ideas", the origin of the hysteresis debate can be traced back at least some twenty years. The aim of this short paper is to acquaint very briefly the reader with the concept of hysteresis and to present an overview of the papers included in this special issue. Nothing new is offered in this skeleton overview, nor is it intended to give a full and detailed survey about all aspects.

The paper is organized as follows. The next section is devoted to a more formal treatment of hysteresis. Section 3 very briefly describes the origin and the history of the hysteresis debate (in other sciences). Section 4 attempts to give an idea about the role hysteresis is playing in economics. Finally, section 5 presents an overview of the papers included in this volume.

[1] I am grateful for helpful comments to G. Heidbrink, J. Möller, H.J. Ramser, W. Scheremet, and W. Smolny (University of Konstanz).
Prof. Wolfgang Franz, Fakultät für Wirtschaftswissenschaft und Statistik, Universität Konstanz, Postfach 5560, 7750 Konstanz 1, FRG.

2 Hysteresis – A Formal Statement

In general terms hysteresis is a property of dynamic systems. Hysteretic systems are path-dependent systems. The long-run solution of such a system does not only depend on the long-run values of the exogenous variables (as usually) but also on the initial condition of each state variable. These systems have a long-lasting memory and are therefore "historical" systems. Loosily speaking: Where you get to is determined by how you get there.[2]

Focussing only on discrete time linear systems hysteresis is present when there are one or more unit roots in the characteristic equation of the state matrix. Consider firstly the simple, one-dimensional case where a variable X_t is subject to the following law of motion:[3]

$$X_t = aX_{t-1} - Z_t, \tag{1}$$

where Z denotes an exogenous variable. If a differs from unity, the steady-state values (denoted by a bar) are:

$$\bar{X} = \frac{\bar{Z}}{(a-1)}. \tag{2}$$

In this case, $\bar{X}$ is unique and independent of the path followed by Z_t, but is solely dependent on the steady-state level $\bar{Z}$.

If, however, a equals unity the steady-state value of X is not unique. The solution of eq. (1) is now given by:

$$\bar{X}_t = X_0 - \sum_{i=1}^{t} Z_i, \tag{3}$$

where we are now considering time dependent values of Z rather than its steady state level.[4] Any value of the steady-state level of X is possible now, because $\bar{X}$ depends on the timepath of Z. This is the case of hysteresis: Any temporary disturbance to Z will have a permanent effect on X.

In the multi-dimensional case x_t is a k-dimensional vector of state variables in time t and z is the respective vector of exogenous variables.[5] The k difference

---

[2] Buiter (1987), p. 24.

[3] See Wyplosz (1987), pp. 124.

[4] In the latter case, eq. (3) is simply $\bar{X}_t = X_0 - t \cdot Z$.

[5] See Möller (1990) for the following considerations.

equations are then given by:

$$x_{t+1} - x_t = \Phi x_t - z_t \tag{4}$$

or:

$$x_{t+1} = \Phi^* x_t - z_t, \tag{5}$$

where Φ denotes the transition matrix and $\Phi^* = I + \Phi$. If all eigenvalues of Φ^* (in absolute values) are strictly less than one, then the difference equation system (4) or (5) is stable. On the other hand, if at least one eigenvalue exceeds unity, the system diverges. Hysteresis occurs if at least one eigenvalue of Φ^* or Φ equals unity or zero, respectively.

For stable systems, applying the steady state conditions:

$$x_{t+1} = x_t \quad \text{and} \quad z_t = \bar{z}. \tag{6}$$

yields:

$$\Phi \bar{x} = \bar{z}. \tag{7}$$

If Φ is not of full rank, the solution of (7) – if it exists – yields multiple equilibria due to linear dependencies between several single difference equations. It can be shown, however, that multiple equilibria do not necessarily imply indeterminacy of the system: If the stability conditions are satisfied there exists a unique stationary equilibrium for any set of initial conditions.[6] The solution of the system (7) is given by [7]:

$$\bar{x} = \Omega_1 x_0 + \Omega_2 \bar{z}, \tag{8}$$

where $\Omega_1 \equiv VQV^{-1}$ and $\Omega_2 \equiv VD^{-}V^{-1}$. The quadratic matrices V and D are of order k and designed to diagonalize Φ so that $\Phi = VDV^{-1}$ holds. The elements of D are zero except the diagonal which contains the eigenvalues of the transition matrix in declining order.[8] The elements of the matrix Q are all zero with the exception of the first element which is a unity matrix.

[6] See Giavazzi and Wyplosz (1985), p. 353 who derive this result for a continuous time model.

[7] For a derivation see Möller (1990).

[8] Accordingly D^{-} is a matrix with zero elements except the i-th diagonal elements which contain the reciprocal non-zero eigenvalues of Φ.

The system (8) reiterates our statement that in the case of hysteresis the steady-state values depend not only on the vector of the exogenous variables, $\bar{z}$, but also on the initial conditions described by $\bar{x}_0$. The non-hysteretic case is obtained for $D^- = D^{-1}$ and all elements of Q being zero so that (8) collapses to the "usual" solution, i.e.,

$$\bar{x} = \Phi^{-1}\bar{z}. \tag{9}$$

The upshot of these considerations can be summarized by the notion that hysteretic systems never forget any shocks even if these have been transitory in nature. They are ultimately responsible for the particular equilibrium (out of many) which the system is approaching.

3 Origins and History of the Hysteresis Debate

The use of the term "hysteresis" has its origins in natural sciences. For example, in biophysics the vibration of biological membranes may follow a hysteresis loop. The expansion and contraction path of arteries may also be subject to hysteresis due to interior frictions. Similar considerations can be found in nonequilibrium thermodynamics within the context of "chemical hysteresis" in the behavior of gas and fluids.[9] Some of these examples bear close relationships to catastrophe theory where a famous example is to establish thresholds for *sudden* behavioral changes of, say, a dog even if the composition of rage and fear is changed only very *smoothly* (the so called "cusp-lines").[10]

In the context of electric engineering the so-called "hysteresis-loop" is a well-known concept to describe the electromagnetic features of ferric metals during a cycle of magnetization and an adjacent period of demagnetization. *Figure* 1 displays a stylized hysteresis loop.[11] Starting in O, the magnetizing force changes the field characteristics to a saturation level (such as B) which is the maximum amount of flux density B that can be forced through a material regardless of the magnetizing force H.[12] Hence, a further increase of the flux density would be inconsequential

[9] More detailed information about the application of the hysteresis phenomenon in natural sciences can be found in textbooks on biophysics such as Hoppe, Lohmann, Markl and Ziegler (1982) from where the aforementioned examples are taken.
[10] See Zeeman (1976), for example.
[11] See Cross and Allan (1988) for a more detailed discussion. Some of the following considerations are also contained in Franz (1989).
[12] See Burke (1986), pp. 63–68 for more details.

for the magnctism of the field. The presence of hysteresis is responsible for the specific way of return of the system if the magnetizing force is removed. Rather than to move back on the original path the system traces back on the upper part of the loop, i.e., on BC and, if the magnetizing force is reversed, on CD, now reaching minus saturation denoted by D. If the magnetic flux is driven again magnetism reaches plus saturation B on the way DFB. Thus, the complete hysteresis loop is given by BEDFB. The original zero-balance of the magnetizing force is now associated with some residual magnetism left in the material denoted by OC or OG, respectively, depending on whether the magnetizing force is decreased from B or increased from D. This residual magnetism is called "remanence". If we are in, say, C the removal of the remanence (in order to restore a zero-magnetic field) requires a further decrease of the magnetizing force of OE (or an increase of OF if we are in G). OE and OF are called "coercivity". The area enclosed by the hysteresis loop indicates the energy loss that will be experienced if the material is cycled in an alternating field. As a consequence of this field-extracted energy the temperature of the cycled material will rise.

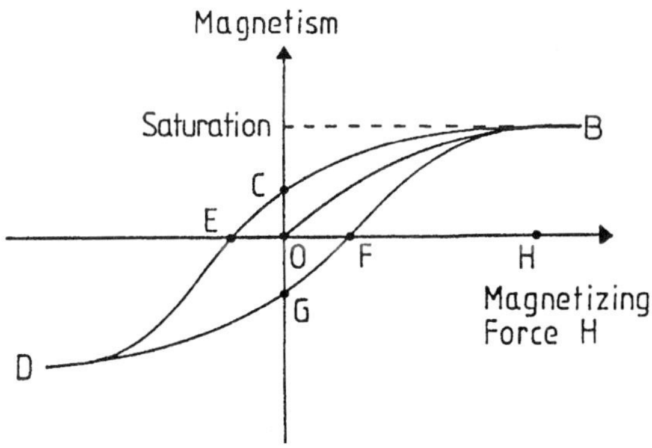

Fig. 1. Magnetic Hysteresis Loop

While a mathematical treatment of the hysteresis loop is beyond the scope of this introduction,[13] the aforementioned considerations carry over to economics with only slight modifications. As an example, simply replace magnetism by "unemployment" and the magnetizing force by an "adverse supply shock" such as the spurt in some raw material prices in the seventies. In the absence of this shock

[13] See the detailed mathematical analysis in the book by Krasnosel'skii and Pokrovskii (1989).

the economy has frictional unemployment O. A certain shock (OH in figure 1) drives unemployment to OB. Removing the shock completely implies a path of unemployment from B to C with OC now representing higher unemployment even though the original supply conditions (e.g., the original oil prices) are prevailing again. Moreover, in order to restore the pre-shock unemployment level a favourable shock of OE would be necessary. The analogy between magnetism and unemployment driven by supply shocks may not be too far reaching but the similarities are obvious. Especially important is the distinction between hysteresis and irreversibility. In contrast to irreversibility, hysteresis does not mean that the process (magnetism, unemployment) cannot be reversed: In magnetism it costs a reduction of magnetizing forces including coercivity to reach the original equilibrium, while in the labor market example this can be restored by removing the adverse supply shock including the allowance for a favourable supply shock.

In physics the hysteresis phenomenon may be traced back to the German physicist Kohlrausch in 1866 and the Scottish physicist-engineer Ewing in 1881.[14] Its explicit use in economics goes back to Samuelson (1965), Georgescu-Roegen (1971), Phelps (1972), and Kemp and Wan (1974).[15] In what follows we discuss these applications in more detail.

4 Hysteresis in Economics

This section is devoted to a brief survey of two major fields in economics in which the hysteresis principle is applied namely in industrial economics with special reference to international trade and in labor economics with special reference to unemployment.

There are other applications of the hysteresis principle which are not reviewed here. For example, in macrodynamics business fluctuations may exhibit hysteresis if an assymmetry of effective demand in ascent and descent is taken into account.[16] While with expansions in output, the expenditures of firms and consumers increase, these expenditures may be reduced less than proportionally with a contraction in output. A related aspect can be found in choice theory where, for example, preferences of consumers change in course of their experiences with consumption, or to quote Georgescu-Roegen: "...in order to determine the equilibrium of the

[14] Source: Cross and Allan (1988), pp. 26–28.

[15] This does not mean that the basic principle of hysteresis was not recognized before. Economists such as R. Frisch, N. Kaldor, and J.A. Schumpeter have been aware of it; see Cross and Allan (1988), pp. 31–35.

[16] See Goodwin and Punzo (1987), pp. 117–124 for more detailed explanations.

consumer (for a fixed budget and constant prices) we need to know more than his particular hysteresis law. Still worse, this law being expressed by a very complex set function, we can only write it on paper but not determine it in actual practice" (1971, p. 126).

4.1 Industrial Economics in an International Setting

As is evidenced in the survey by Kreps and Spence (1985), there is a long tradition in the area of industrial organization pertaining to the role of history in industrial competition. For example, the "immature" stage of industry competition can affect subsequent behaviour and performance in the "mature" stages by tangible variables such as capacity or levels of technical expertise.[17] Another approach to industry dynamics and the role of history in industry maturity is the question to what extent decision-makers have complete rationality. In the case of limited rationality they may adopt rules of thumb by taking into account previous events and situations.

A more direct and worked-out treatment of hysteresis in industrial organization can be found in the field of international trade. Much of the work concerning hysteresis in international trade is done by Richard Baldwin, Avinash Dixit, and Paul Krugman. A good starting point is the paper by Baldwin on "hysteresis in international trade" in this special issue. The basic point is that foreign firms can enter a domestic market only by incurring once-for-all sunk costs. A *temporary* and sufficiently large rise in the exchange rate would induce *permanent* entries by foreign firms. Due to these sunk costs firms will find it profitable to stay in the domestic market even when the exchange rate returns to former levels.[18] Thus, the economy faces quite a different trade pattern although the exchange rate had fallen and ultimately does not differ from its previous value.[19] These considerations are extended in the paper by Baldwin and Krugman (1989) in several ways. Among other aspects, the behavior of aggregated imports is examined when there are many industries subject to potential foreign entry. This aspect is important in order to ensure that the results of the single-industry case do not get smoothed away in the aggregate. Moreover, that paper explicitely deals with the feedbacks from entry and exit decisions to the exchange rate itself. Special attention to hysteretic effects on import prices is drawn by the papers by Baldwin (1988), and Dixit (1989). The argument is that pricing behaviour is affected by the presence of additional foreign firms.

---

[17] These aspects are often dealt with by employing the concept of "learning curves".

[18] See also the study by Fuhrmann (1989).

[19] See also the paper by Bean (1987) for the U.K.

The aforementioned considerations concerning firm behaviour are not restricted to the analysis of international trade. In a more recent paper by Dumas (1989), a general equilibrium framework of capital formation is introduced. To some extent this capital is "perishable" in the sense that it quickly becomes useless if it is left unused for some time, e.g. marketing capital. As in Dixit (1989), an economy with even small setup costs can exhibit a non-negligible hysteresis phenomenon. If the economy with a given distribution of "regular" and "perishable" capital is subject to random productivity shocks there can exist a bifurcating equilibrium in which the economy can equally well embark on a path of sustained positive or negative growth. It all depends on the actual capital mix the economy has been able to achieve.

In a paper by Kemp and Wan Jr. (1974) possible multiplicity of long-run equilibria due to different costs and speeds of adjustments are investigated. While much of the literature focuses on the behaviour of an individual firm which chooses consciously the speed of adjustment, the authors deal with the question as to what extent a whole economy of rationally adjusting firms is affected. The main conclusion of the paper is that if adjustment costs depend on the speed of adjustment "then under positive time preference the position of long-run equilibrium depends crucially on initial conditions – a dramatic example of hysteresis" (p. 222). The basic assumption which creates hysteresis is that at the origin the derivative of the cost-of-adjustment function is discontinuous. Moreover, on the basis of special examples, the possibility of interindustrial wage and marginal productivity differences and, thus, of the path-dependency of long-run equilibria is established.

4.2 Labor Economics

The bulk of recent papers concerned with the hysteresis phenomenon focussed on the persistence of high unemployment in Europe during the 1980s which poses some puzzles for theoretical and empirical macroeconomics. The analytical problems are evidenced by estimates of the "non accelerating inflation rate of unemployment" (NAIRU) which follow the actual path of unemployment rather closely. To put it in R. Solow's words: "A natural rate that hops around from one triennium to another under the influence of unspecified forces, *including past unemployment rates*, is not 'natural' at all." [Solow (1986), p. 533].

It goes without saying, that the analysis of hysteresis in labor economics has forerunners. In 1972 E. Phelps noted that the "natural unemployment rate at any future date will depend upon the course of history in the interim. Such a property is sometimes called hysteresis" [Phelps (1972), p. xxiii]. His example refers to unemployment attributable to the relative size of union wages. An abnormal increase in aggregate demand leads to higher employment of workers not previously belonging to the union even in firms with a union shop. As a consequence, if the union aims to maintain employment of its enlarged membership, it cannot afford to raise the wage rate as much as without this enlargement. Hence, unemployment due to higher union wages is reduced.[20]

As a next landmark, the paper by Hargreaves Heap (1980) should be singled out. The basic point is that the natural rate instead of being at a "level that would be ground out by the Walrasian system of general equilibrium equation" [Friedman (1968), p. 5] is path dependent where the difference between actual and natural unemployment drives the latter. Several ad hoc-arguments are offered for this dynamic dependence such as a depreciation of human capital, a shortage of capital, and the like (see below for a detailed treatment).[21]

It seems fair to say that the revival of the hysteresis debate was put forward by a series of papers by Blanchard and Summers (1986a, 1987). Their model takes up one of the arguments outlined in Hargreaves Heap (1980) and is related to the insider-outsider hypothesis of wage determination emphasized by Lindbeck and Snower (1987). Roughly speaking, the mechanism at work is based on the hypothesis that employed union members (insiders) always set wages so as to maintain just their own employment rather than so as to care for the unemployed (outsiders).[22] Adverse shocks which raise unemployment reduce the number of insiders. The new, smaller group of insiders then forms the basis of the next wage ngotiations. The new, larger group of outsiders has no influence on the bargaining process.[23] Rather, wages are set so as to maintain the new, lower level of employment.[24] The shocks may be temporary but the new, higher level of unemployment is permanent with no tendency to return to its previous, lower level, i.e., unemployment exhibits hysteresis. Obviously, the empirical relevance of this hypothesis rests basically on two premises:[25]

(i) Unions care in fact less about the unemployed outsiders than about the welfare of their employed insiders. In the absence of adequate data which exclusively

---

[20] See Phelps (1972), p. 76–78.

[21] Hansen (1990) and Funke (1990) offer comprehensive surveys of different channals through wich hysteresis effects may work.

[22] See Ramser (1988) for a critical assessment of the insider-outsider theory.

[23] For a similar reasoning see Gottfries and Horn (1988).

[24] The assumption that insiders are to be concerned only with their employment prospects has been called in question by Alogoskoufis and Manning (1988). When they confront various other explanations (such as slow adjustment in the firm's hiring and firing decisions, persistence of wage aspirations of insiders, and the like) with the data for various countries, they find no role for insider membership dynamics.

[25] See Franz (1987), pp. 94 for a more detailed treatment.

refer to insider vs. outsider forces, proxies have been used in aggregate time series regressions on wages such as the distinction between short-term and long-term unemployment where the long-term unemployed are viewed as the outsiders. The empirical results are mixed, however. Layard and Nickell (1986) conclude that most if not all of the pressure on wages in the U.K. comes from short-term unemployment, whereas long-term unemployed exert little influence on wages. By and large, this result is confirmed in the study by Coe (1988) on hysteresis effects in wage equations. Nickell and Wadhwani (1989) in an attempt to assess the relative importance of firm-specific factors (i.e., insider forces) in wage determination also find evidence for insider based hysteresis effects which are, however, inversely related to the extent to which firms take national agreements into account. On the other hand, Holmlund and Zetterberg (1989) in a study for five countries find in their wage equations no evidence in favour of the insider-outsider hypothesis that wages are inversely related to the size of the incumbent work force.

(ii) Unemployed workers cannot find jobs at lower wages outside the unionized sector either because firms do not accept underbidding or because there is no sector that is not covered by collective bargaining. More specifically, employers may refuse to accept such bids due to bowing to social norms according to which underbidding is viewed as an improper form of social behaviour or because the insiders would withdraw cooperation from the underbidders and would "harass" them [Lindbeck and Snower (1988a), p. 167]. This view has been effectively critized on theoretical grounds by Fehr (1990). He shows that given the wage rule assumed by Lindbeck and Snower (1988a) all insiders would be replaced by outsiders. This result may hold even if the wage determination process is changed.

Another mechanism besides wage bargaining which can possibly generate hysteresis stems from the search process seen both from the employer's and the job applicant's viewpoints. To begin with the first, in a screening process the firm has to identify the unknown productivity of the applicant for the job in question. If firms use unemployment experience itself as a screening device, then unemployed persons with a long duration of unemployment are viewed as the less promising candidates due to their (potential) depreciation of human capital during the long unemployment spell. Indeed, in a recent econometric study about the recruitment behavior of firms Ebmer (1989) finds evidence that hiring chances are largely reduced by long-term unemployment as well as by "unfavourable" characteristics such as age, physical disabilities, and the like. Parenthetically we note that some of the long-term unemployed with unfavourable characteristics may have had these attributes already when being employed. Firms may have been reluctant, however, to fire them bowing to social norms and/or because their fellow workers did the work of these persons in order to help them. In the case of bankruptcy or larger dismissals these persons find themselves in the unemployment pool, of course, with virtually no chance to escape from unemployment.

Turning to the other side of the search process long-term unemployed may reduce their search intensity due to their discouragement as a consequence of being so often rejected by employers.[26] Moreover, if skills are acquired not only through on-the-job-training but also through changing jobs, then high unemployment supports a deterioration in skills because it reduces job mobility.[27]

The third major channel through which hysteresis may affect the economy stresses the role of the capital stock. In a neoclassical setting several studies such as Burda (1988) point out that reductions in the capital stock affect labor demand in the same way as adverse supply shocks do. In these models demand shocks have no impact on employment unless they influence the real exchange rate. On the other hand, in a world characterized by price rigidities demand shocks may have a more direct effect on the supply-side capacity. For example, in the model by van de Klundert and van Schaik (1989) an adverse demand shock leads to a reduction in the capital stock if large firms close plants and/or scrap capital. This decrease of the capital stock gives rise to unemployment which may turn out to be persistent because firms cannot suddenly be reopened and begin production even if product demand increases, i.e., the model exhibits hysteresis.

These arguments provide an obvious channel through which hysteresis may affect the NAIRU. The basic idea is that the NAIRU depends on the capital stock.[28] The evolution of the capital stock depends not only on factor prices but also on aggregate demand in the goods market. Running the economy, however, at unemployment rates higher than the NAIRU implies a reduction of investment. This will, in turn, eventually increase the NAIRU. Indeed, econometric estimates of the NAIRU for some countries such as Germany come to the conclusion that especially in the 80s the actual unemployment rate exceeded the NAIRU to a non-negligible extent.[29] Moreover, in the same country capital utilization is above normal. This does, however, not necessarily mean that a possible expansion would be hampered by a capital shortage as long as there are sufficient substitution possibilities between labor and capital and other measures such as an extension of overtime and shift work.

---

[26] On the other hand, long-term unemployed may reduce their reservation wage so that the net effect of the matching process is ambiguous. See Franz and Siebeck (1990) for a theoretical analysis of these aspects within the framework of a theoretical model of the Beveridge curve.

[27] See Hargreaves Heap (1980), p. 614 for this point.

[28] See Sachs (1986) for this argument.

[29] See Schultze (1987) and Franz (1987), for example.

We conclude this subsection with some empirical evidence on hysteresis recently obtained by Gordon (1989). As in other studies the empirical counterpart of the hysteresis phenomenon is a reduced-form equation where the inflation rate (p) as the dependent variable depends on the *change* in unemployment rather than on the *level* of unemployment (U) as in the natural rate hypothesis put forward by Friedman (1968). This can be illustrated very easily using the simplest possible version:

$$p_t = \alpha \cdot p_{t-1} + \beta \cdot (U_t - U_t^*) \tag{10}$$

The NAIRU (U^*) is obtained for a steady-state situation where $p_t = p_{t-1}$. Hysteresis can arise when the NAIRU depends on the history of unemployment, approximated by U_{t-1}, in addition to other (microeconomic) explanatory variables captured by Z_t:

$$U_t^* = \eta \cdot U_{t-1} + \gamma \cdot Z_t. \tag{11}$$

Inserting (11) in (10) and rearranging yields:

$$p_t = \alpha \cdot p_{t-1} + \beta(1-\eta)U_t + \beta\eta\Delta U_t - \beta\gamma Z_t. \tag{12}$$

Full hysteresis occurs if η equals unity, whereas the case $\eta < 1$ is called "persistence".[30] For full hysteresis, we obtain a relation between p_t and the change in unemployment, not the level of unemployment. When we then impose the steady-state conditions and $a = 1$, there is no longer a unique NAIRU. In the other extreme case, if η equals zero, we are left with the standard case where the NAIRU amounts to γZ. Due to a lack of reliable unemployment data for the time period prior to World War I, the unemployment variables are replaced in the study by Gordon with data on detrended log output. As a result for five countries (France, Germany, Japan, U.K., and U.S.) and for the time period 1873–1986 Gordon (1989) concludes that in no country is the hypothesis of *full* hysteresis supported. Only "traces of hysteresis are evident throughout the past century in the form of evidence that prolonged economic slumps have exerted little or no downward pressure on prices in the Unites States and the United Kingdom" (p. 224).[31]

Given some plausibility of the hysteresis or persistence argument, what are the policy implications with respect to labor market issues? If the NAIRU is high be-

---

[30] See Wyplosz (1987), pp. 125–126.

[31] See Graafland (1989) who finds evidence that labor market developments in Europe are more characterized by hysteresis than in the United States.

cause actual unemployment is high, this characteristic renders the NAIRU as a less straightforward guide for economic policy. For example, one might consider making a distinction between a "contemporaneous" NAIRU (i.e., the NAIRU given the history of unemployment) and the steady-state NAIRU (i.e., the NAIRU sustainable in the long-run equilibrium when endogenous responses of the contemporaneous NAIRU to past unemployment are taken into account) [Franz (1987)]. In the presence of hysteresis the contemporaneous NAIRU falls with decreasing actual unemployment as the result of expansionary demand policies.

Does the existence of hysteresis imply that the economy with high unemployment should *always* expand? As has been shown by Sachs (1986) in a theoretical analysis, the answer crucially depends on the initial state of the economy with respect to the level of inflation. If the initial position of the economy is one of low inflation and a high NAIRU – a description which characterizes the economic situation of some countries in the eighties – then an expansion is warranted. On the other hand, if the inflation rate is high and the unemployment rate is moderate, then the optimal path involves rising unemployment and falling inflation. Hence, there is no general case for an expansion in the presence of hysteresis.[32] But if, tax cuts are very likely to be effective according to Blanchard and Summers (1986b). A decrease in tax rates shifts aggregate demand, because of a higher deficit, and aggregate supply, because of the reduction of taxes. Due to the dependence of the subsequent level of wages on the number of insiders, these employment gains (resulting from expansionary policies) are likely to be permanent. Moreover, tax cuts can ultimately increase employment and real wages without spurring government budget deficits.

5 Overview of Papers

How do the contributions written for this special issue fit into the framework outlined in the previous section? All but one of the papers are concerned with labor market issues. This reflects the persistence of high unemployment in Europe during the eighties and the discomfort with the conventional theories of how to explain this phenomenon.

The exception is the paper by Richard Baldwin which deals with hysteresis in international trade. The first draft of this paper was already written in 1986 and, therefore, it represents a major basis of much of the subsequent work on this subject that was surveyed in the previous section. The basic idea is that due to sunk

[32] See Buiter and Gersovitz (1981) for an analysis of dynamic controllability of systems with hysteresis. The interpretation by Sachs (1986) is examined and partly rejected by Möller (1990).

market-entry costs a temporary exchange rate shock can lead to a lasting distortion of comparative advantage.

Is unemployment in Europe plagued by the hysteresis phenomenon? One possible view is that increases in unemployment in Europe over the past decade are attributable to divergences of interests of different groups that cannot be mediated by the marketplace. This is the theme of the paper by Michael Burda which claims that in a democratic model of union wage-setting, monopoly unions can induce hysteresis in the behavior of employment, at least locally. Using unit root tests and Granger causality tests the author concludes that there is little evidence that employment hysteresis constitutes the key difference between the European and the U.S. experiences. On the other hand, trade union membership data from the Federal Republic of Germany provide in this study strong support for the membership hysteresis hypothesis in that country.

As has been documented in the previous section, wage equations may be used to detect the sources of a possible hysteresis effect. David Coe investigates the extent to which wages are determined by insiders, with outsiders having little impact on the wage bargain. Based on a specification which nests alternative models to the wage determination process, the apper presents estimates of wage equations for fifteen industries for fourteen industrialized countries. The results offer support to the insider view of wage determination. Again, hysteresis does not appear to characterize wage formation in the high-unemployment European countries to a greater extent than in North America and Japan.

Rather than to look at wage equations, one can apply other econometric methods to identify possible hysteresis. Albert Jaeger and Martin Parkinson suggest a test for hysteresis in unemployment based on an unobserved components model. Observed unemployment rates are decomposed into a natural rate component and a cyclical component. The impact of lagged cyclical shocks on the current natural component is the measure of hysteresis. The authors find no evidence of hysteresis in U.S. data, whereas German unemployment rates exhibit substantial hysteresis. For both countries, natural rate shocks turn out to be an important impulse mechanism to explain movements in observed unemployment rates.

Another procedure is applied in the paper by Joachim Möller. He focuses on the deterioration of human capital during spells of unemployment. The importance of this aspect has been mentioned in the previous section. In his model the deterioration of human capital during unemployment affects the relation between vacancies and unemployment in a specific way: In the case of labor market slackness the steady state Beveridge curve bends away markedly from the standard u/v-curve. The Beveridge curve may even be upward sloping implying the existence of multiple equilibria. Empirical estimates for Germany reveal that this has been the likely case in that country.

Austria is in many aspects a country which is distinct from other industrialized countries. Since it is included only in the paper by Michael Burda, it seems appropriate to have a closer look. This is done in the contribution by Peter Neudorfer, Karl Pichelmann, and Michael Wagner. Their paper analyses hysteresis or persistence effects in Austrian unemployment data using formal unit root tests and a macroeconometric model of wage-price formation. Their empirical results point towards a considerable amount of persistence in unemployment generated by the rising share of long-term unemployed that has been associated with the increase in overall unemployment in that country.

References

Alogoskoufis G S, Manning A (1988) On the Persistence of Unemployment, Economic Policy 7: 428–469

Baldwin R (1988) Hysteresis in Import Prices: The Beachhead Effect, American Economic Review 78: 773–785

Baldwin R, Krugman P R (1989) Persistent Trade Effects of Large Exchange Rate Shocks, Quarterly Journal of Economics 104: 635–654.

Bean C (1987) Sterling, Misalignment and British Trade Performance, London School of Economics, Centre for Labour Economics, Discussion Paper No. 288 (July), London

Blanchard O J, Summers L H (1986a) Hysteresis and the European Unemployment Problem, in: S. Fischer (ed.), NBER Macroeconomics Annual 1986, Cambridge MA (MIT Press): 15–78

Blanchard O J, Summers L H (1986b) Fiscal Increasing Returns, Hysteresis, Real Wages and Unemployment, NBER Discussion Paper No. 2034 (October), Cambridge MA

Blanchard O J, Summers L H (1987) Hysteresis in Unemployment, European Economic Review 31: 288–295

Brunello G (1988) Hystersis and "the Japanese Unemployment Problem": A Preliminary Investigation, mimeo Osaka University

Buiter W H (1987) The Right Combination of Demand and Supply Policies: The Case For a Two Handed Approach, NBER Working Paper No. 2333, Cambridge MA

Buiter W H, Gersovitz M (1981) Issues in Controllability and the Theory of Economic Policy, Journal of Public Economics 15: 33–43

Burda M (1988) Is there a Capital Shortage in Europe?, Weltwirtschaftliches Archiv 124: 38–57

Burke H E (1986) Handbook of Magnetic Phenomena, New York (Van Nostrand Reinhold)

Coe D T (1988) Hysteresis Effects in Aggregate Wage Aspirations, in: R. Cross (1988): 284–305

Cross R (1987) Hysteresis and Instability in the Natural Rate of Unemployment, Scandinavian Journal of Economics 89: 71–89

Cross R ed. (1988) Unemployment, Hysteresis, and the Natural Rate Hypothesis, Oxford (Basil Blackwell)

Cross R, Allan A (1988) On the History of Hysteresis, in: R. Cross (1988): 26–38

Dixit A (1989) Hysteresis, Import Penetration, and Exchange Rate Pass-Through, Quarterly Journal of Economics 104: 205–228

Dumas B (1989) Perishable Investment and Hysteresis in Capital Formation, NBER Working Paper No. 2930 (April), Cambridge MA

Ebmer R (1989) Some Micro Evidence on Unemployment Persistence, Paper presented at the 4th Annual Congress of the European Economic Association held in Augsburg

Fehr E (1990) Do Cooperation and Harassment Explain Unvoluntary Unemployment? American Economic Review (forthcoming)

Franz W (1983) The Past Decade's Natural Rate and the Dynamics of German Unemployment: A Case Against Demand Policy?, European Economic Review 21: 51–76

Franz W (1987) Hysteresis, Persistence, and the NAIRU: An Empirical Analysis for the Federal Republic of Germany, in: R. Layard and L. Calmfors (eds.), The Fight Against Unemployment, Cambridge MA (MIT Press): 91–122.

Franz W (1989) Das Hysteresis Phänomen, WiSt-Wirtschaftswissenschaftliches Studium 18, No. 2: 77–80

Franz W, Siebeck K (1990) Theoretical Aspects of the Relation between Unemployment and Vacancies, University of Konstanz, Department of Economics, Discussion Paper Nr. 102, Konstanz

Friedman M (1968) The Role of Monetary Policy, American Economic Review 58: 1–17

Fuhrmann W (1989) Außenwirtschaftliche Persistenzen und Wechselkurselastizitäten, Zeitschrift für Wirtschafts – und Sozialwissenschaften 109: 585–602

Funke M (1990) Das Hysteresis-Phänomen, mimeo, Berlin

Georgescu-Roegen N (1971) The Entropy Law and the Economic Process, Cambridge MA (Harvard University Press)

Giavazzi F, Wyplosz C (1985) The Zero Root Problem: A Note on the Dynamic Determination of the Stationary Equilibrium in Linear Models, Review of Economic Studies 52: 353–357

Goodwin R M, Punzo L F (1987) The Dynamics of a Capitalist Economy, Oxford (Basil Blackwell)

Gordon R J (1989) Hysteresis in History: Was There Ever a Phillips Curve?, American Economic Review 79 (Papers and Proceedings): 220–230

Gottfries N, Horn H (1988) Wage Formation and the Persistence of Unemployment, Economic Journal 97: 877–884

Graafland J J (1989) Can Hysteresis Explain Different Labour Market Operations between Europe and the United States? Applied Economics 21: 95–111

Hansen G (1990) Die Persistenz der Arbeitslosigkeit. Eine theoretische und empirische Analyse, in: G. Nakhaeizadeh and K.-H. Vollmer (eds.), Neuere Entwicklungen in der angewandten Ökonometrie, Heidelberg (Springer), forthcoming

Hargreaves Heap S P (1980) Choosing the Wrong Natural Rate: Accelerating Inflation or Decelerating Employment and Growth, Economic Journal 90: 611–620

Holmlund B, Zetterberg J (1989) Insider Effects in Wage Determination: Evidence from Five Countries, Uppsala University, Department of Economics, Working Paper No. 11/1989, Uppsala

Hoppe W, Lohmann W, Markl H, Ziegler H (1982) Biophysik, 2nd. ed, Berlin (Springer)

Kemp M C, Wan H. Y Jr (1974) Hysteresis of Long-Run Equilibrium from Realistic Adjustment Costs, in: G. Horwich and P.A. Samuelson (eds.), Trade, Stability, and Macroeconomics, New York (Academic Press): 221–242

Klundert Th van de, Schaik van A (1989) Unemployment Persistence and Loss of Productive Capacity: A Keynesian Approach, Paper presented at the 4th Annual Congress of the European Economic Association held in Augsburg.

Krasmosel'skii M A, Pokrovskii A V (1989) Systems with Hysteresis, Berlin (Springer)

Kreps D M, Spence A (1985) Modelling the Role of History in Industrial Organization and Competition, in: G.R. Feiwel (ed.), Issues in Contemporary Microeconomics and Welfare, London (MacMillan): 340–378

Layard R, Nickell S (1986) The Performance of the British Labour Market, London School of Economics, Centre for Labour Economics, Discussion Paper No. 249 (September), London

Lindbeck A, Snower D J (1987) Efficiency Wages Versus Insiders and Outsiders, European Economic Review 31: 407–416

Lindbeck A, Snower D J (1988a) Cooperation, Harassment, and Involuntary Unemployment: An Insider-Outsider Approach, Amercian Economic Review 78: 167–188

Lindbeck A, Snower D J (1988b) The Insider-Outsider Theory of Employment and Unemployment, Cambridge MA (MIT Press)

Möller J (1990) Das Hysteresis Phänomen in Arbeitslosigkeit-Inflations-Modellen: Theorie, Empirische Relevanz und wirtschaftspolitische Konsequenzen, mimeo, Konstanz

Nickell S, Wadhwani S (1989) Insider Forces and Wage Determination, London School of Economics, Centre for Labour Economics, Discussion Paper No. 334 (January), London

Phelps E S (1972) Inflation Policy and Unemployment Theory, London (Macmillan)

Ramser H J (1988) Lohnbildung und Beschäftigung: Anmerkungen zur Relevanz des Insider-Outsider-Ansatzes, in: Universität Konstanz, Fakultät für Wirtschaftswissenschaften und Statistik (ed.), Zum Gedenken an Harald Gerfin, Konstanz: 55–69

Sachs J D (1986) High Unemployment in Europe: Diagnosis and Policy Implications, NBER Working Paper No. 1830 (February), Cambridge MA

Samuelson P A (1965) Some Notions on Causality and Teleology in Economics; reprinted in: The Collected Scientific Papers of Paul A. Samuelson, Vol III: 428–472

Schultze Ch L (1987) Real Wages, Real Wage Aspirations, and Unemployment in Europe, in: R.Z. Lawrence and Ch.L. Schultze (eds.), Barriers to European Growth. A Transatlantic View, Washington D.C. (Brookings Institution): 230–291

Solow R M (1986) Unemployment: Getting the Questions Right, Economica 53 (Supplement): 523–534

Wyplosz C (1987) Comment on W. Franz: "Hysteresis, Persistence, and the NAIRU. An Empirical Analysis for the Federal Republic of Germany", in: R. Layard and L. Calmfors (eds.), The Fight Against Unemployment, Cambridge (MIT-Press): 123–131

Zeeman E C (1976) Catastrophe Theory, Scientific American 234, part 4, 65–83

Hysteresis in Trade[1]

By R. Baldwin[2]

Abstract: The paper presents a model of hysteresis in trade which is based on the existence of sunk market-entry costs. The study concentrates on the aspect of two models. In both models an exchange rate overvaluation leads to additional entry by foreign firms. The models differ in their accounts of why the foreign firms do not exit after the exchange rate shock passes.

1 Introduction

This paper presents a model of hysteresis in trade that is based on the existence of sunk market-entry costs. Since the first draft of this paper was presented in April 1986, a number of studies have extended and amplified the sunk market-entry cost idea. Baldwin and Krugman (1989) allow for a stochastic exchange rate and show that hysteresis in trade leads to hysteresis in the equilibrium exchange rate. Baldwin (1988) shows that the sunk cost model might account for the behavior of US import prices. Dixit (1989a and 1989b) solves the sunk cost model assuming a Brownian motion exchange rate process and is able to parameterize hysteresis in terms of the underlying volatility of the exchange rate. Krugman (1988) suggests that there is a vicious cycle between hysteresis and exchange rate volatility. The motivation for models of hysteresis in trade stems primarily from the puzzling behavior for US trade during the 1980s.

The recent overvaluation of the dollar and the resulting loss of US competitiveness has elicited a great deal of re-thinking among economists, politicians and businessmen about the relationship between exchange rates and trade. One of the most often heard allegations is that some of the inroads made by foreign firms in the US market during the overvaluation will remain even after the dollar returns to its old purchasing power parity level. For instance a recent New York Times article (July 14, 1986) remarked that:

---

[1] I gratefully acknowledge the helpful comments and suggestions of Harry Foster, Steve Postrel, Paul Krugman and Gene Grossman. Prepared for the NBER Summer Institute, 1986, International Studies.

[2] Richard Baldwin Columbia University 611Uris Hall, New York, NY. 10027, USA.

> … the industries of countries that established big stakes in the American market appear unwilling to give them up. In the past they would raise their prices in line with the decline of the dollar, but no longer. Now they are willing to shave profits to remain competitive here.

Standard trade theory would predict that the falling dollar would decrease U.S. net imports, although with a lag. What the above allegation asserts is that the strong dollar has resulted in a shift in the relationship between the exchange rate and imports. The effect of this claim, if it turns out to be valid, would be to force a rethinking of the welfare effects of floating versus fixed exchange rates. Moreover, it would have implications for optimal exchange rate adjustment policies and for commercial policy during cyclical exchange rate movements. Lastly it would require a revision of the static concept of an equilibrium exchange rate.

Hysteresis is the name for this "history matters" property. While the normative aspects of hysteresis mentioned above are perhaps the most important, they cannot be properly handled without a positive theory of the phenomenon. This paper concentrates on the positive aspects of two models of hysteresis in trade. In both models an exchange rate overvaluation leads to additional entry by foreign firms. The models differ in their accounts of why the foreign firms do not exit after the exchange rate shock passes.

The first difficulty in modeling hysteresis in trade is to construct a model in which the exchange rate affects trade. Exchange rates in simple general equilibrium trade models are irrelevant, due to the standard assumptions of market clearing and no assets. However, when we allow for tradeable assets and floating exchange rates, the current account has little impact on the current exchange rate. This is true, a fortiori, for the trade balance of any single industry. It therefore seems reasonable to ignore the general equilibrium feedback that imports have on the exchange rate. To this end, this paper works with partial equilibrium models and takes the exchange rate as exogenous.

Given the exogeneity of exchange rates, an overvaluation lowers foreign firms' marginal costs (in dollars) relative to those of domestic firms. In almost any model this reduction would lead to greater imports. The key to hysteresis is that the augmentation of imports outlasts the temporary overvaluation. Therefore the key to any model which displays hysteresis is the source of persistence. There are basically two possible channels by which a shock can lead to persistence. In the first an exogenous shock causes long-lived changes in the structure of the economy. The second is based on the existence of multiple equilibria. In this genre of models, the shock leads to hysteresis by shifting the economy from one equilibrium to another. This paper studies a model of each type. Before presenting the models formally, we review their principal features and informally sketch out the basic economics underlying them.

The first model is based on fixed selling costs that are sunk and durable. Suppose that in order to sell in a country, a firm must expend some resources in setting up a distribution and service network. While some of these costs may be recouped if the firm ceases to sell in the country, some of them are likely to be sunk costs. That is, incurring the fixed costs is a pre-condition to selling in the country but once they are incurred they need not be repeated nor can they be recovered. One of the best examples of sunk and durable selling costs is firm-specific human capital. Both the management and the service network staff must acquire market-specific training which is also firm-specific. Given this, a firm contemplating entering the US market must expect to receive a price sufficiently above its variable costs to cover its sunk costs.

Now in an imperfectly competitive world with these fixed costs, consider the effects of a prolonged overvaluation of the dollar. The high dollar will reduce the dollar value of foreign firms' marginal costs. Other things equal this will increase the market shares and profits of foreign firms. Greater profits will in turn lead more foreign firms to make the investment necessary to sell in the US market. However, since the investment is durable and sunk, not all of the new entrants will exit when the exchange rate returns to its pre-overvaluation level. Thus the US market will be more competitive and imports will be higher after the shock is over. It could be argued that this sort of effect has influenced the evolution of the automotive industry in recent years. Since 1981 many new foreign firms have entered the US car and small truck market. Having already invested in advertising and distributorships, the new Japanese and Korean companies may find it profitable to continue to sell in the US despite the weakening dollar.

The second model is based on multiple equilibria. In the presence of increasing returns to scale, the number of firms that can operate in a market without losing money is finite and is determined endogenously (assuming free entry). The nationality of the firms, however, is not in general determinate. For instance, in the extreme case where foreign and domestic firms have identical costs, only the total number of foreign and domestic firms taken together is determinate. Any allocation of this number between foreign and domestic firms constitutes an industry equilibrium. In this model an exchange rate shock could knock the economy from one equilibrium to the other and thus result in hysteresis in trade. It is conceivable that this sort of effect has influenced the evolution of the semiconductor industry in recent years.

The term hysteresis seems to have been introduced to the trade literature by Kemp and Wan (1974). Krugman (1986) considers the implications of hysteresis in the trade balance for the *PPP* level of the dollar. He does not model hysteresis explicitly, but offers dynamic economies of scale as a possible explanation for the existence of hysteresis in trade. Kemp and Wan construct a closed economy model of hysteresis which relies on firms' cost of adjusting their labor forces. They also conjecture that their model could be modified to account for hysteresis in trade patterns due to international labor migration. A recent model with hysteresis can be found in Blanchard and Summers (1986). These authors find empirical evidence of hysteresis in European unemployment rates. They present a model of this hysteresis based on an institutional argument concerning labor union behavior. The idea of selling expenses as a barrier to entry dates back at least to Williamson (1963). Foster and Baldwin (1986) studies the implications that marketing investments have on the relationship between exchange rates and domestic prices. The models presented below follow the basic approach of Dixit (1979, 1980) and Eaton and Lipsey (1980, 1981).

A third possible model of hysteresis, which is not worked out here, relies on demand side factors. The idea is based on imperfectly informed consumers. Suppose consumers are uncertain about the quality of goods they have never tried. Moreover assume that the only way to ascertain the quality of a product is to actually consume it. Goods that have these characteristics are often referred to as experience goods. Now suppose that the consumers' beliefs about the quality of an untried product follow a certain distribution. Additionally assume that the mathematical expectation of the distribution is correct in that it reflects the true quality of an untried product. Faced with the choice of tried and untried products which are objectively of the same quality, the consumer will be willing to pay more for the known brand since it involves no uncertainty.

The effect of this demand structure is that new entrants face an initial period of low demand during which consumers become familiar with their product. Suppose furthermore that firms must incur some fixed costs in order to sell in the domestic country (these costs need not be sunk or durable). In this framework, a firm will enter the domestic market only if it anticipates that the sum of its operating profits in both the introductory and established periods will cover its fixed costs.

It is easy now to see how this combination of fixed costs and demand structure can lead to persistences. An overvaluation means higher operating profits for prospective foreign entrants during the overvaluation. Ceteris paribus, this allows more foreign firms to cover the fixed cost of selling in the domestic market. When the exchange rate returns to its pre-overvalued level, the foreign marginal costs rise. However, since domestic consumers have tried their products, foreign firms also face higher demand curves. Consequently it is possible that not all the new entrants will be forced out. Essentially the shock leads to a lasting change in the information sets of consumers. This structural change leads to hysteresis.

The first section of the paper puts forth a model of a Cournot duoploy in which the basic results of hysteresis and its welfare implications can be examined. Section two looks at some testable implications of the sunk and durable selling costs idea in a slightly more general Cournot oligopoly model. The third section considers the exchange rate path necessary to un-do the hysteresis generated by a temporary overvaluation. The last section examines multiple equilibria as a source of hysteresis in trade.

2 Hysteresis in a Cournot Duoploy

The model we adopt in this section is a version of the familiar Cournot duopoly model with sequential entry.[3] The model has only three periods. The period zero equilibrium is taken as given and plays the role of an initial condition. We trace through the effects of an exchange rate change over periods 1 and 2. There are only two firms. The incumbent firm is assumed to be a domestic firm. The only prospective entrant is a foreign firm. The firms produce identical products.

The choices faced by the foreign firm are first whether to enter or not, and then the level of sales to the home market in each period if entry is chosen. Since the incumbent (domestic) firm has already entered, its only choices are its output quantities in periods 1 and 2. The period-by-period post-entry equilibrium concept employed is Cournot-Nash. That is to say, each firm chooses its output to maximize profits taking the other firm's output as given. The resulting multi-period equilibrium will be sub-game perfect. The behavior of the domestic and foreign firms in other markets is ignored.

The foreign firm's entry decision occurs at the beginning of period 1. The foreign firm enters the domestic market only if it anticipates that the present discounted value of its revenues are sufficient to cover its costs. Issues of expectations are potentially quite important, however to concentrate on hysteresis in trade we assume that all firms have perfect foresight on all variables. In this section we also ignore the issue of exit by assuming that the sunk costs are "immortal", to use Eaton and Lipsey's terminology.

Production of the good by both firms is subject to the same constant average variable cost, c, where the units of c are the domestic currency for the home firm and foreign currency for foreign firms. To sell in the home market a fixed cost, F, must be incurred in addition to the direct production costs.[4] The sunk and durable fixed costs, F, are incurred in the domestic country and so are unaffected by the exchange rate. This cost is meant to reflect firm-specific selling costs such as the costs of setting up a distribution and service network, establishing a brand name through advertising, and mangers' learning how to sell in a new market. Also included in these costs are the investments necessary to bring the foreign product in conformity with the domestic health and safety regulations. The assets acquired through the expenditure of F are assumed to be entirely firm-specific. Their re-sale value therefore is zero.

---

[3] See the models of Dixit (1979, 1980) and Eaton and Lipsey (1980, 1981).

[4] Allowing the home and foreign firms to face different F's would complicate the analysis without providing any compensating insight. If F were larger for the foreign firm than for the home firm, it would simply take a larger appreciation to induce the foreign firm to enter (by inspection of equation (3)).

The costs of the domestic firm in domestic currency units are thus, $c((x_1/R) + (x_2/R^2)) + F$, where $R = (1 + r)$, r is the discount rate and x_1 and x_2 are sales in periods 1 and 2. The costs for the foreign firm in domestic currency is $c((e_1y_1/R) + (e_2y_2/R^2)) + F$, where y_i and e_i are the period i sales of the foreign firm and the exchange rate defined as domestic currency units per foreign currency unit. The inverse demand function in period i is linear, namely $p_i = a - \beta(x_i + y_i)$.

Putting these assumptions together, the problem of the domestic firm is to choose x_1 and x_2 to maximize $\sum_i [(p_i - c)x_i / R^i] - F$. The summation runs over the first and second periods. If the foreign firm enters, its problem is to choose y_1 and y_2 to maximize $\sum_i [(p_i - ce_i)y_i / R^i] - F$.

A. The Benchmark Case

As a benchmark, we first consider the case of a constant exchange rate fixed at unity. When the exchange rate equals unity, the two firms face equivalent marginal costs (*EMC*). If the foreign and home countries are symmetric, the *EMC* exchange rate is also the purchasing power parity (*PPP*) exchange rate.

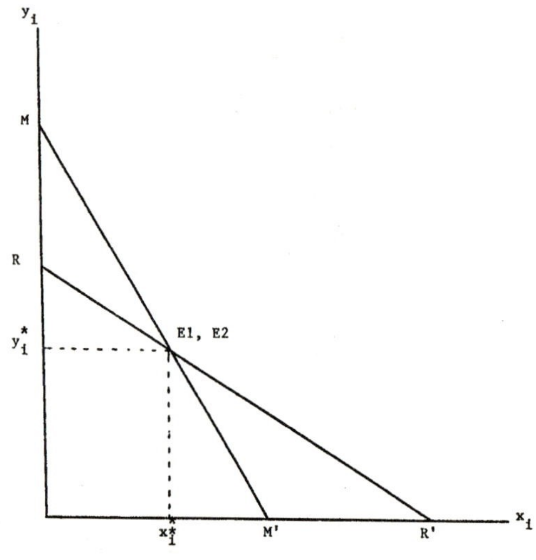

Fig. 1.

Since there are only two firms, yet we wish to examine the effects of foreign entry in response to exchange rate movements, we assume that the taste and cost parameters are such that there is only room for one firm (the domestic firm) in the benchmark case. The standard solution technique for this sort of multi-period Cournot game is to work backwards. Namely, we provisionally suppose that entry occurs and then work out the equilibrium outputs in periods 1 and 2 for both the incumbent and the entrant. We then ask whether the entrant would find entry profitable given the equilibrium outputs.

Figure 1 faclitates the analysis. The line *MM´* gives the domestic firm's best response function in period *j*. The equation for *MM´* is the first order condition of the incumbent's problem taking the foreign firm's output as given:

$$x_j = \left(\frac{\alpha - c}{2\beta}\right) - y_1 / 2, \qquad j = 1, 2. \tag{1}$$

Likewise the best response function for the foreign firm is graphed as *RR´*. Its equation is:

$$y_1 = \left(\frac{\alpha - ce_j}{2\beta}\right) - x_j / 2, \qquad j = 1, 2. \tag{2}$$

The post-entry Cournot equilibrium in period 1 is the intersection of the two best response functions, *E*1. The output of the incumbent is x_1^* and that of the entrant is y_1^* The period 2 equilibrium, *E*2, is identical to the period 1 equilibrium since by assumption $e_2 = e_1 = 1$.

To find conditions implied by the assumption that only the domestic firm operates, we check whether the present discounted value of the foreign firm's operating profits over the two periods would cover the sunk costs *F*. Here operating profits are defined as current revenue less current variable costs. With the assumption of linear demand, it is easy to show that operating profits for the foreign firm in period *i* are $O\Pi_\iota = \beta(y_1^*$. Algebraically the foreign firm will not enter if for $e_2 = e_1 = 1$:

$$F > [(\alpha - ce_1)^2 / 9\beta R] + [(\alpha - ce_2)^2 / 9\beta R^2]. \tag{3}$$

The condition under which the domestic firm makes non-negative profits as a monopolist is: $F \leq [(a - ce_1)^2 / 4\beta]((1 / R) + (1 / R^2))$. Obviously for some values of a, c and β, the domestic firm will find it profitable to operate while the foreign firm will not. Discounting plays no role in the hysteresis in this model. For simplicity's sake then, we ignore it by assuming that $R = 1$.

B. Temporary Overvaluation

Having established the benchmark case, we consider the effects of a temporary overvaluation of the exchange rate. The thought experiment we run is the following. In period zero the exchange rate is unity and the domestic firm is a monopolist as in the benchmark case. In period 1 the exchange rate appreciates to e_1 ($e_1 < 1$) and then returns to unity in period 2. We shall be concerned with the effects of the overvaluation on the foreign firm's decision to enter and thereby on its effects on imports.

As before we work out the equilibrium backwards. The post-entry period 2 equilibrium is plainly identical to the benchmark equilibrium. In period 1, however, the foreign firm has a relative marginal cost advantage and thus we should expect it to take a larger share of the market. The situation is shown in Figure 2. The best response functions in period 2 are MM' and R_2R_2' and those in period 1 are MM' and R_1R_1'. Clearly if the overvaluation is large enough, the foreign firm's period 1 sales (and therefore its profits) will be large enough to cause it to enter. The formal condition is that e_1 is small enough so that for $e_2 = 1$ the inequality (3) fails to hold. We assume that this is the case so that the foreign firm enters.

An immediate consequence of the entry is that the relation between the exchange rate and imports is now altered. In the benchmark case, the *EMC* exchange rate elicited an import level of zero. After the temporary overvaluation, however, the *EMC* exchange rate results in positive imports equal to x_2^* in Figure 2. Algebraically this level of imports equals $(a - c) / 3\beta$. Clearly then entry results in hysteresis in trade.

Intuitively, the temporary deviation from the *EMC* exchange rate level leads to larger operating profits for the foreign firm during the overvaluation. This in turn allows the foreign firm to cover the sunk costs of selling in the home market. The new entry makes the domestic market more competitive. Prices and domestic profits in both period 1 and 2 are lower than in the benchmark case. Moreover output and employment in the domestic industry are lower, even after the shock has passed.

To highlight the economics of this model we note that the crucial element in the model is the fact that the investment is sunk and durable. Having assumed that the investment is also a fixed cost, additional investment occurs only through the entry of additional firms. Nevertheless, in a slightly different model in which there was some substitutability between the investment and other factors of production, hysteresis could result from increased investment by foreign firms who had already entered.

Welfare results are always model dependent and therefore subject to qualification. In this paper, I ignore adjustment costs, external economies of scale and dynamic economies of scale. All these factors would tend to make temporary overvaluations welfare-worsening. With this caveat in mind, we turn to the standard welfare implications of hysteresis as measured by the sum of consumer and producer surplus. In the traditional trade model, a temporary overvaluation is simply a favorable shift in the terms of trade. To focus on the welfare impact of hysteresis itself (rather than that of the temporary overvaluation), we compare home country welfare before and after the temporary overvaluation. As a point of reference we note that the traditional trade model presumes that the trade pattern returns to its previous state after the exchange rate shock passes. Consequently, it would predict that there would be no change in consumer and producer surplus.

The proximite cause of the hysteresis is an increase in the number of foreign firms in the domestic market. This in turn results primarily in a redistribution of welfare. Prices are lower so consumers are better off. The domestic firm owners, however, are worse off since domestic profits are lower. The net welfare impact of the exchange rate movement is, in general, ambiguous due to the Brander and Spencer (1983) logic. In the special case considered above, it is easy to show that the sum of domestic consumer surplus and pure profits falls.

In this model changes in e_1 are isomorphic to a foreign export subsidy. Brander and Spencer (1985) point out that such a subsidy could harm domestic welfare by shifting rents from home firms to foreign firms. So our result is really an application of the Brander-Spencer logic. However, Eaton and Grossman (1985) point out that the Brander-Spencer welfare results are highly sensitive to assumptions about the strategic interactions between the firms. Hence our results are likely to be sensitive to the particular assumptions made about strategic behavior.

3 Testable Implications

The simple, explicit model in the last section served to highlight the mechanism by which sunk and durable selling costs could lead to hysteresis in trade. While the model contains many highly special assumptions, even this simple model can generate some interesting, testable implications. In this section, we introduce a Cournot oligopoly model and show that the model implies a positive correlation between a measure of hysteresis and the size of sunk selling costs in cross-sectional data.

The key to the hysteresis is the presence of the sunk and durable selling costs. Intuitively then we might expect larger sunk costs to lead to "more" hysteresis. In the duopoly model, the point is easily made. If F is small enough, there is room for both firms even in the benchmark case. The temporary overvaluation would therefore not cause any additional entry. Consequently there would be no hysteresis. Obviously the two firm assumption is too artificial in this context. To redress this, we consider a Cournot oligopoly model.

When we shift to the oligopoly model we maintain all of the assumption of the section I model, except of course the assumption that there is only room for one firm in the benchmark case. Therefore the parameters in the following equations are to be taken as distinct from those in the preceding sections. The equilibrium can be calculated with the help of a figure similar to Figure 2. The equations for the best response functions are more complicated. For home firms it is now:

$$x_4 = \left(\frac{\alpha - c}{\beta(m+1)}\right) - \left(\frac{m}{n+1}\right) y_1, \qquad i = 1, 2, \tag{4}$$

where m and n are the number of foreign and domestic firms. Likewise for foreign firms it is:

$$x_4 = \left(\frac{\alpha - c}{\beta(m+1)}\right) - \left(\frac{m}{n+1}\right) y_1, \qquad i = 1, 2. \tag{5}$$

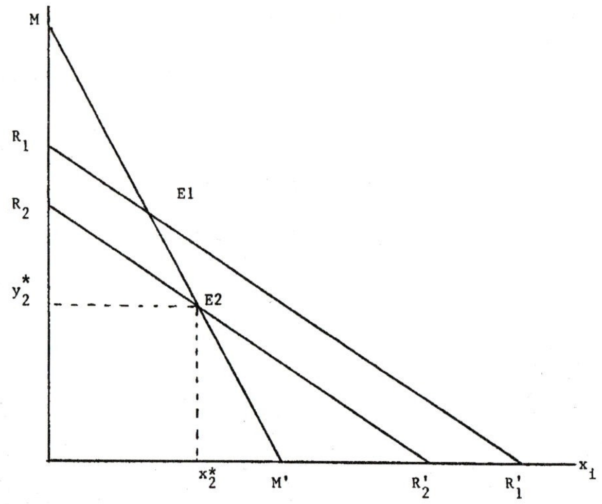

Fig. 2.

The equilibrium is calculated as before, but we must now also determine the equilibrium number of firms. The entry condition for firms is the same as before. We start by determining the period zero equilibrium number of firms. Because the cost functions of foreign and domestic firms are identical in period zero, only the sum, $m + n$, can be solved for. Any particular division of this sum into domestic and foreign firms provides our initial conditions. Specifically we take $m = m^\circ$ and n $= n^\circ$ in the period zero equilibrium. The overvaluation favors foreign firms at the expense of domestic firms. There is thus no pressure for n to increase in periods 1 and 2. Having ruled out exit, n cannot decrease in periods 1 and 2. Consequently the period 1 and 2 equilibrium number of domestic firms is n°. On the other hand, the equilibrium m in periods 1 and 2 will be greater than m°. Ignoring integer constraints, we can calculate the free entry, perfect foresight m for periods 1 and 2 by solving the foreign firms' zero profit condition for m in terms of the cost parameters, the demand parameters, e_1 and n°.

As in the section I model, the temporary overvaluation makes the domestic market more competitive. This results in domestic prices and profits that are lower in period 2 than they were in period zero. As in the duoploy case the welfare impact is in general ambiguous. Nonetheless, given the Cournot assumption, the sum of domestic producer and consumer surplus can be shown to decrease when no is greater than m°. That is to say, when the industry is dominated by domestic manufacturers, the lost profits outweigh the gains to consumers. A temporary overvaluation is therefore welfare worsening. Again, it is important to note that this result is probably quite sensitive to the Cournot assumption.

To quantify hysteresis, we want a measure of the magnitude of the change in the relationship between imports and the exchange rate. To this end we define H as the difference between the import level corresponding to the EMC exchange rate with and without the temporary overvaluation. That is $H = m'y_2'^{*} - m^{\circ}y_2^{\circ *}$ where the variables with noughts are from the benchmark case and those with primes are from the temporary overvaluation case. Plugging in the equilibrium values for m', $y_2'^{*}$, m° and $y_2^{\circ *}$ the formula for this measure reduces to:

$$H = (2^{-1/2} - [1 + (y_1'^{*} / y_2'^{*})^{-1/2})(n+1)(F / \beta)^{1/2}. \tag{6}$$

Since $y_1'^{*} > y_2'^{*}$, the model predicts that after a temporary overvaluation H will be larger in industries with large sunk selling costs. Thus for example we should expect H to be larger in industries for which after-sales service is important, such as motor vehicles and electrical equipment. Practically, H might be taken as the difference between the actual level of imports and the level of imports predicted by an estimated import equation.[5]

Another empirical implication is that import price elasticities are not structural. In other words, we should observe structural breaks in the time series estimates of import equations that are correlated with large movements in the exchange rate. The models in this paper ignore adjustment costs and expectation formation processes. The level of imports predicted by the models does not, therefore, depend on past values of the exchange rate. In practice, however, all import equations include lagged relative price and income terms. The exact empirical implications of the structural break are therefore somewhat unclear. The model definitely predicts a struc-

---

[5] H measures the difference between imports with and without the new entrants. Empirically import volume equations are usually estimated as log-log functions of domestic income (or expenditure) and the relative price of imports (plus lags). Hysteresis shifts the relationship between imports and the right hand side variables and so would look like a structural break. H, then, is simply the forecast error from a standard import volume equation.

tural break in the current relative price coefficient. To determine how the additional foreign entry affects the lag structure would require specifying the microeconomics of the lag.

4 Corrective Undervaluations

If the recent high US dollar has actually caused hysteresis in some industries, a natural question is the following: How far must the dollar fall to restore import shares to their pre-overvaluation level? For instance, controlling for changes in comparative advantage, how high must the Yen-US dollar rate go to restore the Japanese share of the US car market to its 1981 level?

In the section I and II models, a temporary overvaluation leads to a *permanent* change in the zero-imports exchange rate level. This result is too extreme. More sensibly we might expect that the hysteresis might fade away or could be undone by an extended undervaluation. Equation (2) shows that imports are negatively linked to the contemporary exchange rate. To restore our model to its initial equilibrium, however, the undervaluation must do more than reduce the sales of foreign firms. It must actually force out the new entrants. To study this aspect of hysteresis, we run another thought experiment. We ask: Given a period 1 overvaluation large enough to induce entry, what must the period 2 exchange rate be in order to restore the exchange rate-import relationship to its pre-overvaluation state? Before turning to the model, note that the assumption of perfect foresight is not innocuous when the possibility of exit exists.[6]

To run this thought experiment, we find it convenient to add an additional period to the oligopoly model. Thus we suppose that $e_0 = 1$, $e_1 < 1$, $e_2 > 1$ and $e_3 = 1$. We must also confront the issue of exit. Exit is a difficult concern and has still not been thoroughly explored in the literature.[7] The first problem is now to define exit. Clearly since the fixed costs are sunk in the simple model, a zero sales level in any period is not a useful definition of exit. Instead we shall define exit as the removal of the assets corresponding to the sunk costs, F.

We can get a handle on the exit problem by first considering the extreme case. Suppose that as in the Section I and II models, the marketing investment never depreciates. In this case the asset can never be un-sunk and therefore a temporary overvaluation will result in a permanent change in the relation between exchange rates and imports. While this polar case is lacking in realism, it serves to bring out

[6] If firms are uncertain about future exchange rates then the sunk assets have an options value that is not reflected in operating profits.

[7] See Eaton and Lipsey (1980, 1981) and Ghemawat and Nalebuff (1984) for discussions of exit.

the importance of the durability of the sunk asset emphasized by Eaton and Lipsey (1980).

More realistically we might assume that the asset depreciates. Exit could then be defined to occur gradually as the foreign firm's ability to sell in the home market deteriorated. This approach however is not easily incorporated into our model since the sunk costs are also fixed. The tack that we shall adopt is in the spirit of the depreciation approach. Specifically we assume that in order to continue selling in the home country, firms must incur a fixed maintenance cost G in each period. If G is not spent the sunk asset disappears. for instance if F represents the cost of a brand-name introduction advertising blitz, G would represent the brandname maintenance advertising.

In the light of these extensions, the foreign entry occurs if $\beta[(y_1^*)^2 + (y_2^*)^2 + (y_3^*)^2] + > (F + 2G)$, or $\beta[(y_1^*)^2 + (y_2^*)^2] > (F + G)$. The conditions for exit to occur in period 2 is that $\beta[(y_2^*)^2 + (y_3^*)^2] < 2G$. In other words, the firm exits if the profits it anticipates cannot cover the maintenance costs on the sunk asset.

Consider the implications of these extensions for the thought experiment. First note that the second period undervaluation necessary to bring about exit depends on the size of the maintenance costs, G. Thus for example if G is large enough, it is possible that no undervaluation at all is needed to restore the system. In other words, a simple return to the *EMC* exchange rate in periods 2 and 3 could bring about the requisite exit. One immediate implication fo this is that the under- and overvaluations need not in general be symmetrical.

Another point is that the greater the overvaluation, the greater must be the depreciation required to undo its effects. This can be seen from the solution of (4) and (5). It is easy to show that the partial derivative of y_i^* with respect to e_i is decreasing in m. In other words, the impact of an exchange rate fall on foreign firms' operating profits is diminished by higher values of m. Since the amount of entry, and thus m, is positively linked to the size of the overvaluation, the smaller is e_1, the greater m will be. Consequently the size of the corrective fall in the exchange rate increases with the size of the overvaluation.

5 Multiple Equilibria Hysteresis

The hysteresis in the previous sections was caused by a lasting change in the market structure of the industry. An entirely separate source of hysteresis is the presence of multiple equilibria. In the first section, it was assumed that there was room for only one firm. We further assumed that the incumbent firm was domestic. Another equilibrium would have resulted if the incumbent had been foreign. Owing to this possibility, there is a fundamental indeterminancy in the model. Formally the indeterminancy was removed by taking the period zero equilibrium as given. It is clear though that in the section I model history matters in a manner entirely apart from the sunk and durable costs.

This point can be seen more clearly in a modified Section I duopoly model. Suppose that F is fixed but not durable. Namely, suppose that a firm must expend $F/2$ in each period in order to sell in the home market. In this model, we start with the domestic firm as the incumbent and examine the effects of a temporary overvaluation. The post-entry equilibrium sales are the same as in Figure 2. However now a firm will choose zero sales in any period in which it cannot cover the fixed costs $F/2$. If the overvaluation is large enough, x_1^* will be small enough so that $\beta[(y_1^*)^2 < F/2$. Plainly then the domestic firm would choose zero sales in period 1 and the foreign firm would become a monopolist. Now when the exchange rate returns to its *EMC* level in period 2, there is only room for one firm. However that firm is now the foreign firm. Obviously this model is subject to hysteresis. It is important to note that this form of hysteresis leans rather heavily on the assumption of Cournot behavior (this point is discussed below).

Since the hysteresis stems from the existence of multiple equilibria rather than the durability of investments, there is no tendency for the hysteresis to fade. In the modified Section I model the firms have identical costs at the *EMC* exchange rate. There are therefore no factors that would force the economy back to the period zero equilibrium. Nevertheless, a corrective undervaluation could undo the hysteresis. That is, an undervaluation that gave the domestic firm a relative cost advantage could return the economy to the period zero equilibrium.

The welfare results and policy implications of multiple-equilibria hysteresis are straightforward. This type of hysteresis is unambiguously welfare worsening. The period 2 price is unchanged by the overvaluation so consumers are unaffected. However, domestic profits are zero, so that domestic firm owners lose. This indicates that cyclical commercial policy could improve domestic welfare. That is to say, the domestic country could increase its welfare by imposing a tariff during the temporary overvaluation. The cyclical tariff, however, need not completely offset the overvaluation. It need only be large enough to make foreign entry un-profitable.

As mentioned above, the assumption of Cournot behavior in this model is more than just a convenient way of modeling imperfect competition. Alternatively, the domestic firm might conjecture that increasing its output would cause the foreign firm to greatly curtail production. In this case it is possible that the domestic firm would re-gain its monopoly status in period 2 and hysteresis would therefore not occur. Moreover, if the domestic firm could credibly commit to re-entering in period 2, the foreign firm would find it optimal to exit and again the hysteresis result would disappear.

An example can provide another way to highlight how strong the Cournot assumption is in the context of this model. The model implies that a temporary exchange rate shock can lead to a lasting distortion of comparative advantage. That is, with Cournot behavior, an exchange rate shock might result in domination by the foreign producers, even if the foreign industry had a cost disadvantage. More sensibly, if an overvaluation lead to domination by the high cost foreign firm, we might expect a war of attrition to result. In other words, if the foreign firm has a relative cost disadvantage, the monopolist position is worth more to the domestic firm than it is to the foreign firm. In a set-up that allowed for more periods, the domestic firm might find it rational to endure negative profits for a few periods in order to force out the foreign firm.

Clearly further research is needed to clarify these issues. Nonetheless, based on these informal arguments, it seems that the range of industries in which multiple-equilibria hysteresis could be important is circumscribed. First of all, this sort of hysteresis could be important in industries where domestic and foreign industries have approximately the same costs. Secondly it could be important in industries which manufacture products with short product life cycles. In such industries it is unlikely that a war of attrition would be a profitable strategy.

Another assumption that is crucial to hysteresis in the above models is increasing returns to scale. Casual observation suggests that most of the new foreign products sold in the US were produced and sold overseas before the strong dollar. In other words the foreign entry did not involve the creation of new firms or products but rather an expansion in the foreign firms' marketing areas. This indicates that the only fixed costs relevant to hysteresis are those involved in marketing in the domestic economy. Nonetheless in certain industries, such as the semiconductors and electronics, new products and companies have emerged during the overvaluation. If the domestic market represents a significant fraction of world demand then the fixed costs of production would be sufficient to yield hysteresis. It could be argued that the evolution of the semi-conductor industry was affected by exchange rate induced hysteresis.

References

Baldwin R (1986) "Hysteresis in Trade", MIT mimeo prepared for 1986 NBER Summer Institute, April

Baldwin R (1988) "Hysteresis in Import Prices: the Beachhead Effect", *American Economic Review*, September, 78

Baldwin R, Krugman P (1989) "Persistent Trade Effects of Large Exchange Rate Shocks", Quarterly Journal of Economics

Brander J, Spencer B (1985) "Export Subsidies and International Market Share Rivalry", *Journal of International Economics*, 18, 227–242

Blanchard O, Summers L (1986) "Hysteresis and the European Unemployment Problem", *NBER Macroeconomic Annual*, 1

Dixit A (1980) "The Role of Investment in Entry-Deterence", *The Economic Journal*, 90, 95–106

Dixit A (1979) "A Model of Duopoly Suggesting a Theory of Entry Barriers", *The Bell Journal of Economics*, Spring, 20–32

Dixit A (1989a) "Entry and Exit Decisions Under Uncertainty", Journal of Political Economy, 97, 3, p. 620

Dixit A (1989b) "Hysteresis, Import Penetration, and Exchange Rate Pass-through", Quarterly Journal of Economics

Dornbusch R (1976) "Expectations and Exchange Rate Dynamics", *Journal of Policitcal Economics*, 84: 1161–76

Eaton C, Lipsey R (1980) "Exit Barriers are Entry Barriers, the Durability of Capital as Barrier to entry", *The Bell Journal of Economics*, 11, 2, 721–729

Eaton C, and Lipsey R (1981) "Capital, Commitment and Entry Deterence", *The Bell Journal of Economics*, 12, 2, 593–604

Eaton J, Grossman G (1985) "Optimal Trade and Industrial Policy Under Oligopoly", *Quarterly Journal of Economics*, 100, 383–406

Foster H, Baldwin R (1986) "Marketing Bottlenecks and the Relationship between Exchange Rates and Prices", MIT mimeo, October

Ghemawat and Nalebuff (1984) "Exit", Harvard Institute of Economic Research, No. 1069

Kemp M, Wan A (1974) "Hysteresis of Long Run Equilibria from Realistic Adjustment Costs", in *Trade, Stability and Macroeconomics*; *Essays in Honor of Lloyd Metzler*, G. Horwich and P. Samuelson (eds), Academic Press, 1974

Krugman P (1986) "Is the Japan Problem Over?", MIT mimeo, April

Williamson O E (1963) "Selling Expense as a Barrier to Entry", *Quarterly Journal of Economics*, 112–128

Some Evidence on the Membership Hysteresis Hypothesis in Europe

By M. C. Burda[1]

Abstract: In a democratic model of union wage-setting, monopoly unions can induce hysteresis in the behavior of employment, at least locally. As a result, autoregressive representations of employment and membership should contain a unit root even if the determinants of labor demand are stationary. In addition, the model predicts that employment should Granger-cause consumption wages. These implications are tested with data from several European countries. Although there is little conclusive evidence that employment hysteresis constitutes the key difference between the European and US experiences, trade union membership data from the Federal Republic of Germany provides strong support for the membership hysteresis hypothesis in this country.

1 Introduction

Recent discussion of unemployment in Europe has focused on the roles of insiders and outsiders in wage determination.[2] In this view, high European unemployment is not so much due to deficient aggregate demand *per se* as to the inconsistency of wages chosen by the collective bargaining process with labor market clearing. Insiders – those who hold jobs, belong to unions, or possess some form of local monopoly power – do not care sufficiently about outsiders – the unemployed and new labor force entrants. Consequently, unemployment inherits the temporal dynamics of this insider group; adverse unanticipated shocks to labor demand, re-

---

[1] This paper is based on some results of Chapter 3 of my PhD dissertation at Harvard University. In an effort to pay off some old debts, I would like to thank J.T. Dunlop for timely financial assistance as well as Olivier Blanchard, David Levine, Warwick McKibbin, Changyong Rhee, Larry Summers and seminar participants at Harvard, Texas, Wisconsin, Cornell, Chapel Hill, the Board of Governors of the Federal Reserve System, and the 1987 NBER Summer Workshop for useful comments and suggestions. The comments of two referees on the current version are also gratefully acknowledged. André Urani assisted with the computations.
Michael C. Burda, INSEAD, F-77305 Fontainebleau.

[2] See Lindbeck and Snower (1984), Solow (1985), Blanchard and Summers (1986), and Gottfries and Horn (1987).

gardless of their source, can reduce the number of insiders and induce a reoptimization of wage policy with respect to the new, smaller group. Blanchard and Summers (1986) have associated this „membership effect“ with attenuated mean-reversion or hysteresis in employment and unemployment in European economies.

This paper evaluates some implications of the membership hysteresis hypothesis for a number of West European economies. It motivates these implications using Burda's (1987, 1990) dynamic extension of Blair and Crawford's (1984) social choice model of union behavior. This framework explicitly addresses the role of seniority in the allocation of jobs, and thus captures some aspects of heterogeneity in membership that are lost in hiring hall models of union behavior (McDonald and Solow 1981, Oswald 1982, Blanchard and Summers 1986, Gottfries and Horn 1987). Second, it attempts to evaluate empirically the first link in the „insider-outsider“ account of persistently high unemployment in Europe: that adverse shocks to employment over the last decade have permanently altered the path of union wage demands and subsequent employment.

While the concept of „membership“ has several interpretations (Blanchard and Summers 1986), the role of trade unions themselves in such an account must play a central role in distinguishing US and European labor markets. Whereas unions are involved in the determination of wages for less than 20% of employment in the US, the percentage of employees whose wages are directly or indirectly determined in collective bargaining exceeds 75% in most major European economies.[3] The role of these institutional differences is supported by considerable cross-country evidence on nominal and real wage behavior (Perry 1975, Spitäller 1976, Gordon 1977, 1982; Sachs 1979, Bruno and Sachs 1985).

Our findings, however, offer only limited support for the notion that insider-outsider phenomena have been important in explaining low frequency movements in European employment. While the weak implication of a unit root in the univariate autoregressive representation of the employment process is not rejected by European data, the stronger prediction that employment Granger-cause real wages is only supported consistently for the United States. Exploiting a data set on union membership from the Federal Republic of Germany, however, we find some weak evidence for the hysteresis hypothesis in this economy.

The rest of the paper is organized into three sections. Section 2 analyzes a dynamic model of a democratic union with endogenous membership, whose members differ by a seniority ranking. This model yields the membership hysteresis result. Section 3 motivates the empirical tests applied to European and US data and presents the results. The last section offers some tentative conclusions.

---

[3] See Blythe (1979), Faxén (1982), Flanagan et.al. (1983), Bruno and Sachs (1985).

2 Wage Setting in Unions with Endogenous Membership: The Hysteresis Result[4]

Consider a monopoly union consisting of M members, which sets wages for all workers employed in a particular industry or economy. To simplify matters, we assume initially that it can set real consumption wages, i.e., that it can forecast the price level perfectly. The only source of worker heterogeneity – and divergence of preferences – is a seniority ranking on the positive ray.[5] Employment is allocated (hires and fires are made) on a LIFO basis with respect to order in the seniority queue; a worker with seniority rank S is employed at the union wage W if labor demand L exceeds S, otherwise he receives some alternative level of utility which is taken as given.

The union faces a competitive industry of wage-taking firms which choose employment unilaterally after the wage is set. We thus model partial equilibrium in the labor market, as the union perceives no effects of the wage-employment outcome on output price, demand, or outside alternatives. Employing the convention of denoting natural logarithms with lower case letters, we let the industry demand for union employment in period t be given by the constant elasticity specification:

$$\ell_t = \varepsilon_t - \eta w_t \,, \tag{1}$$

where ℓ is union employment and ε is a random demand shifter. The constant elasticity of demand η may be broadly interpreted as subsuming the effects of underbidding by outsiders. Since w is the log *consumption* wage, ε subsumes several sources of uncertainty that shift the labor demand curve: shocks to total factor productivity, the effective capital stock, or the price ratio of consumption goods to the price of output. The union sets w before observing ε, but knows it mean ε and the distribution of its expectational error ν. Ignoring integer issues, the probability of union employment Π_t for a worker of seniority ranking s is

$$\begin{aligned} \Pi_t &= \text{Prob}[\ell_t > s] \\ &= \text{Prob}[\varepsilon_t - \eta w_t > s] \\ &= \text{Prob}[\varepsilon_t - E_{t-1}\varepsilon_t > s - E_{t-1}\varepsilon_t + \eta w_t] \\ &= 1 - F(s - E_{t-1}\varepsilon_t + \eta w_t)\,, \end{aligned} \tag{2}$$

---

[4] This results presented here are derived in Burda (1990).

[5] For two earlier static models of seniority unions, see Blair and Crawford (1984) and Grossman (1983).

where F is the cumulative distribution of ν. The composite random shock ε is assumed to follow an AR (1) process:

$$\varepsilon_t = \rho\varepsilon_{t-1} + \nu_{t'} \tag{3}$$

with $|\rho| \leq 1$, and ν iid with zero mean.[6] It follows that $E_t\varepsilon_{t+i} = \rho^i\varepsilon_t$, $i = 1, 2, \ldots$ where E_t denotes expectation conditioned on period t information.

The distribution function of ν, F, rarely takes a form that allows closed form solution of the model. However, the existence of a median voter equilibrium in seniority requires it to have a nondeclining hazard rate.[7] We make the following approximation:

$$F_0 + F_1z + .5F_2z^2 \qquad F_0, F_1, F_2 > 0\,. \tag{4}$$

A union member of seniority s in period t, then, has employment probability

$$\Pi_t = 1 - F_0 - F_1(s - E\varepsilon_t + \eta w_t) - .5F_2(s - E\varepsilon_t + \eta w_t)^2\,. \tag{5}$$

As in Blanchard and Summers (1986), we approximate expected utility in each period as linear in log consumption wages w and the (level) probability of employment, Π:

$$EU = w + \gamma\Pi \tag{6}$$

---

[6] It should be noted that (3) may be generalized to an nth order autoregressive process written in the form

$$\tilde{\varepsilon}_t = \tilde{\rho}\tilde{\varepsilon}_{t-1} + \tilde{\nu}_t,$$

with $nx1$ vectors $\tilde{\varepsilon}_t \equiv [\varepsilon_t \ldots \varepsilon_{t-n+1}]'$, $\tilde{\nu}_t \equiv [\nu_t, 0 \ldots 0]$ and $\tilde{\rho}$ the $(n \times n)$ matrix

$$\begin{bmatrix} \rho_1 & \rho_2 & \cdots & \cdots & \cdots & \rho_n \\ 1 & 0 & 0 & \cdots & \cdots & 0 \\ 0 & 1 & 0 & \cdots & \cdots & 0 \\ \vdots & & & & & \vdots \\ 0 & 0 & 0 & \cdots & 1 & 0 \end{bmatrix}$$

Now (1) becomes $\ell_t = i'\varepsilon_t - \eta w_t$, where $i = [1 \quad 0 \ldots 0]'$.

[7] See Blair and Crawford (1984) or Burda (1987) for a discussion.

with $\gamma > 0$. Burda (1987) has shown that (6) is a linearization of expected utility around some steady state value of Π when utility is isoelastic and the replacement ratio is constant.

The crucial element of a dynamic model of union membership links the group in whose interests the union are maximizing to actual employment. We initially consider a union shop that automatically extends permanent membership to new employees, which includes the seniority rating s. That is,

$$m_t = \ell_t \tag{7}$$

The membership votes at the end of the period on the next period's wage. Since hiring and firing are done on a LIFO basis, the employment probability Π provides a unique ranking of the unemployed or „outsiders" who have ever worked. This facilitates analysis of expected utility as an „outsider" and eliminates the necessity of the „once an outsider, forever an outsider" assumtion found in Blanchard and Summers (1986).

Solution for the wage rule proceeds by backwards recursion from a terminal period T. In period $T - 1$, the expected utility of a worker with seniority s is

$$w_T + \gamma \Pi_T \tag{8}$$

with

$$\Pi_T = 1 - F_0 - F_1(s - \rho\varepsilon_{T-1} + \eta w_T) - .5F_2(s - \rho\varepsilon_{T-1} + \eta w_T)^2. \tag{9}$$

Note that there is no unanimity and hence no „representative member" in this union. The union's preference ordering over wages is assumed to be the outcome of majority voting; alternatively, a democratically elected leadership is assumed to maximize its reelection chances by implementing the majoritarian preferences of voting members. Since the choice set of the membership is unidimensional (wages), a voting equilibrium á la Sen (1970) will exist if preferences over wages are single-peaked for any arbitrary seniority level s, which is guaranteed effectively by the restrictions on F_0, F_1, and F_2. It follows that the most preferred policy of the median voter will defeat all other policies in a series of pairwise contests. The union will set w_T to maximize the utility of the worker with median seniority log $(M/2) = m - \log 2$; i.e., solve

$$\max_{w_T} \, [w_T + \gamma \Pi_T] \tag{10}$$

subject to

$$\Pi_T = 1 - F_0 - F_1(m_{T-1} - \log 2 - \rho\varepsilon_{T-1} + \eta w_T) \\ - .5F_2(m_{T-1} - \log 2 - \rho\varepsilon_{T-1} + \eta w_T)^2 \,. \tag{11}$$

The most preferred wage for the median voter, denoted by an asterisk, is

$$w_T^* = (1/\eta)[\rho\varepsilon_{T-1} - m_{T-1} + \log 2 + (1 - \gamma F_1 \eta)/\gamma F_2 \eta] \,. \tag{12}$$

Already the one-period case highlights the important role of membership in wage setting. Blanchard and Summers (1986) and Gottfries and Horn (1987) have derived a similar relationship between membership and wages in a hiring-hall union model, in which the probability of employment is the same for all members. Both models imply that movements in membership affect the optimal union wage, *ceteris paribus*. If adverse unanticipated shifts in labor demand induce a reduction in membership, the new optimal union wage is higher, looking in a level of employment that might have been considered „slack“ by the old membership. Involuntary unemployment arises whenever the voting membership does not equal the market clearing level of employment.

In period $T-2$, a worker with seniority index s understands the outcome of the period $T-1$'s voting equilibrium, and incorporates the $T-1$ median voter's most preferred policy w_T^* in his evaluation of alternative wages in $T-1$. If β $(0 < \beta < 1)$ is the discount factor, expected utility conditioned on $T-2$ information (ε_{T-1} is not yet known) is

$$E_{T-2}[w_{T-1} + \gamma[1 - F_0 - F_1(s - \rho\varepsilon_{T-2} + \eta w_{T-1}) \\ - .5F_2(s - \rho\varepsilon_{T-2} + \eta w_{T-1})^2] \\ +\beta[w_T^* + \gamma[1 - F_0 - F_1(s - \rho\varepsilon_{T-1} + \eta w_T^*) \\ - .5F_2(s - \rho\varepsilon_{T-1} + \eta w_T^*)^2]] \tag{13}$$

Note that the probability of employment in T in the maximand (13) is different for each level of seniority. By inspection, the function (13) upon substitution of (12) remains single-peaked in the current wage w_{T-1}, so the union maximizes the expected utility of median voter/worker, in $T-2$, solving

$$\max_{w_{T-1}} E_{T-2}[w_{T-1} + \gamma[1 - F_0 - F_1(m_{T-2} - \log 2 - \rho\varepsilon_{T-2} + \eta w_{T-1}) \\ - .5F_2(m_{T-2} - \log 2 - \rho\varepsilon_{T-2} + \eta w_{T-1})^2] \\ + \beta[w_T^* + \gamma[1 - F_0 - F_1(m_{T-2} - \log 2 - \rho\varepsilon_{T-1} + \eta w_T^*) \\ - .5F_2(m_{T-2} - \log 2 - \rho\varepsilon_{T-1} + \eta w_T^*)^2]]]$$

subject to (12). The first order condition is

$$E_{T-2}[1-\gamma F_1\eta-\gamma F_2\eta(m_{T-2}-\log 2-\rho\varepsilon_{T-2}+\eta w_{T-1}))$$
$$+\beta(\partial w_T^*/\partial w_{T-1})[1-\gamma F_1\eta-\gamma F_2\eta(m_{T-2}-\log 2-\rho\varepsilon_{T-1}+\eta w_T^*)]]]=0\,. \quad (14)$$

Inspection of (12) with $m_{T-1} = \ell_{T-1}$ reveals $\partial w_T^*/\partial w_{T-1} = 1$; substitution of w_T^* and m_{T-1} and rearranging yields the rule

$$w_{T-1}^* = (1/\eta)[\rho\varepsilon_{T-2} - m_{T-2} + [\log 2 + (1-\gamma F_1\eta)/\gamma F_2\eta]/(1+\beta)]\,. \quad (15)$$

The structure of the problem guarantees a voting equilibrium at each point of recursion. The optimal wage for $T-N$, $N>0$ is given by

$$w_{T-N}^* = (1/\eta)\{\rho\varepsilon_{T-N-1} - m_{T-N-1}$$
$$+[\log 2 + (1-\gamma F_1\eta)/\gamma F_2\eta]/(1+\beta+\ldots+\beta^N)\}\,.$$

Letting $N \to \infty$ and resubscripting such that $t = T - \infty$, we obtain the following time-invariant wage rule, or „target wage“:

$$w_t^* = (1/\eta)[\rho\varepsilon_{t-1} - m_{t-1} + (1-\beta)[\log 2 + (1-\gamma F_1\eta)/\gamma F_2\eta]]\,. \quad (16)$$

Finally, the implied employment process can be derived given (16) and (1):

$$\ell_t = \ell_{t-1} - (1-\beta)[\log 2 + (1-\gamma F_1\eta)/\gamma F_2\eta] + v_t\,. \quad (17)$$

Employment follows a random walk with drift which is independent of ρ, the serial correlation of shocks to labor demand. The sign of drift term $-(1-\beta)$ $[\log 2 + (1-\gamma F_1\eta)/\gamma F_2\eta]$ will depend on the relative weight of wages and the probability of employment in utility (γ), the elasticity of labor demand (η), as well as the response of Π to w (parametrized by F_1 and F_2). The greater the elasticity of labor demand, the relative utility of job security, and the sensitivity of job security to the wage, the more positive the drift.

The drift term is also inversely related to β, approaching zero as $\beta \to 1$. In words, the more highly the median voter values future relative to current utility, the more likely he will favor wage setting that maintains his expected position as median voter in the next period. If $\beta = 0$ (members are myopic or extremely impatient), the solution is the same as in the fixed membership case. Wage setting is more moderate when voting membership is variable than when it is fixed, and if member workers value future utility.[8] Thus, in addition to factors described by Blair and

[8] A similar result obtains in Blanchard and Summers (1986).

Crawford (1984) and Farber (1986), „Cheshire Cat" behavior of seniority unions implied by a negative drift term in (17) will be retarded if members have a sufficiently high discount factor.

The assumption that voting membership equals current employment is probably unrealistic; labor unions in most European countries retain unemployed members on their books for some time after they lose their jobs.[9] Burda (1990) solves for the time-invariant wage policy rule when voting membership instead equals a Koyck distribution of lagged employment:

$$m_t = \lambda \sum_{i=0}^{\infty} (1-\lambda)^i \ell_{t-i} \qquad 0 < \lambda < 1. \tag{18}$$

where λ is the short-run elasticity of membership with respect to employment. The solution, which is obtained by the method of undetermined coefficients, is

$$w_t^* = (1/\eta)[\rho\varepsilon_{t-1} - m_{t-1}] + \Phi \tag{19}$$

where Φ is a constant that depends on λ as well as β, γ, F_1, F_2, and η.[10] Employment will now follow the process

$$\begin{aligned} \ell_t &= m_t + \eta\Phi + v_t \\ &= \lambda \sum_{i=0}^{\infty} (1-\lambda)^i \ell_{t-i-1} + \eta\Phi + v_t. \end{aligned} \tag{20}$$

Wages are set so that the expected value of employment equals membership plus a constant drift term. Since the coefficients on employment in the membership rule sum to unity, the autoregressive representation of employment process will contain a unit root.[11]

The implications of a seniority union for wage and employment dynamics are similar to those discussed by Blanchard and Summers (1986), who considered a hiring hall union with variable membership. First, the union wage rule induces a unit root in the process followed by employment. Second, unions will not consciously induce low profitability through „wage rigidity". If an adverse shock to the labor demand schedule is anticipated, the union will accept wage cuts to protect the current membership. At the same time, unions will raise wages in response to any

---

[9] See Eurostat, Trade Union Membership 1985, for descriptions of union membership rules in Common Market economies.

[10] Burda (1990) shows that $d|\phi|/d\lambda \leq 0$.

[11] The characteristic equation for the autoregressive part is $1 - z(1 - \lambda) / (1 - \lambda z) = 0$, which has one root at $z = 1$.

anticipated favorable shift in labor demand and capture rents for themselves.[12] Third, if labor supply is inelastic and the union effectively sets wages for all workers, the model implies a nonstationary natural rate of unemployment. After a shock, a new membership results, future deviations from which will occur only to the extent that workers are „surprised“ by a productivity or terms of trade disturbance.[13]

Our formulation differs somewhat from the hiring-hall model. First, it allows for heterogeneity and conflict within the union, and has operating characteristics of most industrial trade unions in Western economies.[14] In a hiring hall union, all employees have the same probability of dismissal. Second, because any given median voter is effectively allowed to „decide“ the wage only once, the problems of arbitrary assumptions about utility as an outsider can be avoided. The median voter today need only forecast the wage policy rule of future median voters, which in the current setup is stationary. Third, we are able to characterize the dynamics of employment for more complicated membership rules.

3 Econometric Evidence for the Membership Hysteresis Hypothesis

The model of seniority based labor unions with dynamic membership and democratic voting yields testable implications for the time series of employment, wages, and union membership that we investigate in this section. Unlike Blanchard and Summers (1986) we do not estimate Phillips curves but prefer to test less parametrically-based implications of the membership hysteresis hypothesis.

3.1 Tests for Unit Roots in the Autoregressive Representation of Employment

In an influential paper, Nelson and Plosser (1982) stressed the pitfalls of deterministic trend estimation when unit roots are present in the autoregressive representation. Tests have been developed to detect the presence of unit roots in the

---

[12] This implication was anticipated long ago by Simons (1944).

[13] Note that the last conclusion is not entirely at odds with more traditional models of union wage setting which stress the rigidity of wages in times of adverse shocks to labor demand. The important distinction is between anticipated and unanticipated shocks.

[14] See Oswald (1984), Abraham and Medoff (1985), and Oswald and Turnbull (1987). The widespread European institution of works councils often make firing older workers relatively more expensive for the firm by linking severance benefits to tenure. Soltwedel (1984) describes possible effects of such institutions in West Germany.

context of specification search; when theory predicts that time series under consideration possess this form of nonstationarity, these diagnostic tools can also serve as tests of the relevant model.

According to (17), employment will follow a random walk with drift, independent of the AR(1) process followed by the labor demand shock ε. For the more general membership rule (18) the autoregressive representation of employment will contain a unit root; that is, the polynomial in the lag operator will have a root on the unit circle. This would suggest employing an augmented Dickey-Fuller test similar to that used by Nelson and Plosser (1982). The null hypothesis that X_t is a univariate integrated autoregressive process IAR$(1, p)$, is tested against the alternative that X_t consists of a linear time trend t plus a stationary AR$(p + 1)$ process. Under the null, the „*t*-statistic" τ of a in the regression

$$\Delta X_t = \alpha_0 + \alpha X_{t-1} + \sum_{i=0}^{p} \alpha_i \Delta X_{t-i-1} + \alpha_{\text{TIME}}\, t + u_t \tag{21}$$

will have a non-standard distribution for which Fuller (1976) has reported critical values.

The issue of power of these tests remains unresolved. In their novel application of the test to macro variables, Nelson and Plosser (1982) conceded its low power against trend-deterministic alternatives with a highly autoregressive component. Using Monte Carlo methods, Poterba and Summers (1988) demonstrate that conventional significance levels for hypothesis testing (ie 5%) imply a considerable overweighting of Type I errors. They suggest significance levels as high as 40% to compensate for low power. Unfortunately, published tables of the Dickey-Fuller (empirical) distribution do not exist. We take the somewhat arbitrary value of –2.5 as the cutoff point for the t-statistic on the lagged level (in Fuller 1976, –3.0 corresponds roughly to a significance level of 10%).

Equation (21) was estimated with annual observations on manufacturing and total employment for the United Kingdom, France, the Federal Republic of Germany, Italy, Denmark, Sweden, Norway, Austria, and the United States over the period 1952–88.[15] For all countries, $p = 0$ was sufficient to remove serial correlation in the residuals as evidenced by the Q-statistic at eight lags. The results are displayed in Table 1, and show little evidence against unit roots in either manufacturing or total employment for the examined, especially when „conventional" significance levels are considered ($\leq 10\%$). Choosing instead –2.5 as a critical value, we reject a unit root for both US manufacturing and total employment, but also for total

[15] Manufacturing data are annual indices of dependent employment published by the Office of Productivity and Technology of the US Bureau of Labor Statistics. Total employment data are from Grubb (1984), updated when necessary using OECD data.

employment in Germany and Sweden. The unit root results thus offer only weak evidence for hysteresis, and do not differentiate very well between high and low unemployment countries. For example, it is surprising that Austria, whicn is generally considered a „corporatist" economy, exhibits unit root behavior in both employment series.[16]

3.2 Evidence from Vector Autoregressions of Manufacturing Consumption Wages and Employment

A second, potentially more powerful set of tests examines the statistical plausibility of zero restrictions on lag polynomials of vector autoregressions involving real (consumption) wages and employment. Since our model implies that union labor supply is shifted by changes in membership but is perfectly elastic in the current period, employment will under fairly general conditions contain information useful in forecasting future wages. To motivate this, one must model the evolution of *ex post* real consumption wages.

Consider again the *ex ante* optimal wage set by a union with a Koyck membership rule discussed in the previous section:

$$w_t^* = (1/\eta)[\rho\varepsilon_{t-1} - m_{t-1}] + \Phi$$

We define w_t as the realized (observed) consumption wage, allowing now for unanticipated movements in price level: $w_t = w_t^* + \xi_t$. Unions are presumed to have rational expectations, so $E_{t-1}\xi_t = 0$. Now

$$w_t = (1/\eta)[\varepsilon_{t-1} - m_{t-1]} + \Phi + \xi_t \,. \tag{22}$$

After substitution of the voting membership rule (18) for m_{t-1} and $(\ell_{t-1} + \eta w_{t-1})$ for ε_{t-1} in (22) we obtain

$$w_t = (1/\eta)[\rho(\ell_{t-1} + \eta w_{t-1}) - \lambda \sum_0^\infty (1-\lambda)^i \ell_{t-i-1}] - \Phi + \xi_t$$

or,

$$w_t = \rho w_{t-1} + (1/\eta)[\rho \ell_{t-1} - \lambda \sum_0^\infty (1-\lambda)^i \ell_{t-i-1}] - \Phi + \xi_t \tag{23}$$

---

[16] It should, however, be noted that other macroeconomic models – such as the real business cycle model – also predict unit root behavior in aggregate data.

Table 1. Dickey-Fuller tests for a unit root in AR representations of employment, 1952–1988*

Country	Values of τ for: Manufacturing employment	Total employment
UK	–1.752	–2.373[2]
France	0.795[1]	–1.544[1]
FR Germany	–2.342	–2.774
Italy	–0.125[1]	–1.123[3]
Denmark	–1.778	n.a.
Sweden	–1.653	–2.966
Norway	–0.211[1]	n.a.
Austria	–2.165[4]	–1.597[4]
United States	–2.510	–2.6461

* τ is the ratio of the estimate of a to its estimated standard error in equation (21) for $p = 0$. See text for discussion; * and ** denote significance at the 5% and 1% level respectively. Critical values for two-sided test from Fuller (1976, Table 8.5.2) 10%: (–3.00,0.0); 5%: (–3.33,0.34); 1%: (–3.75, 0.72).

[1] Sample ends in 1987. [2] Sample ends in 1985. [3] Sample ends in 1984. [4] Sample ends in 1983.

Table 2. F-tests of $A_{12}(L) = 0$ in VARs of log employment and real consumption wages, 1955–1985

	First differences $k = 3$	First differences $k = 4$	Levels with time trend $k = 3$	Levels with time trend $k = 4$
UK	1.07	0.76	1.01	0.83
France[1]	1.22	1.07	3.52*	3.88*
FR Germany	1.27	1.76	3.96*	2.54
Italy[1]	0.28	0.78	1.10	0.97
Denmark	1.03	1.05	2.80	1.82
Sweden	0.89	0.58	1.75	1.38
Norway[1]	1.05	0.76	3.00*	2.16
Austria[2]	2.08	1.91	1.49	1.25
United States	7.21**	6.08**	4.22*	3.29*

* significant at 5% level; ** significant at 1% level; k is the order of the VAR.

[1] Sample ends in 1987. [2] Sample ends in 1984.

If follows from (23) that employment should be Granger causally prior to (Granger-cause) real consumption wages. Geary and Kennan (1982) find no systematic relationship between employment and real wages in twelve OECD countries, but they employ a deterministic detrending procedure, which may be inappropriate. In contrast, Bruno and Sachs (1985) find systematic statistical links between (product) wages and employment, but stress the direction of the former to the latter.

Table 2 reports Granger causal priority tests at annual frequencies of lagged log employment with respect to real log consumption wages for all countries examined in Table 1. For each country, real consumption wages were measured as weekly compensation divided by respective consumer price indices was obtained from the US Bureau of Labor Statistics.[17] The equations were estimated in first differences and in log levels with a linear time trend. We examined the F-statistics of $A_{12}(L) = 0$ in third and fourth order vector autoregressions of the bivariate system

$$Z_t = A_0 + A(L)Z_{t-1} + e_t \tag{24}$$

where $Z_t = [\Delta w_t, \Delta \ell_t]'$, A is a matrix of polynomials in the lag operator L, and e_t is a (2 x 1) vector of white noise disturbances. Evidently, only US manufacturing data consistently reject the null at conventional significance levels, although there is some support for the model in the log level plus trend equation for Germany, France, and Norway. Because (23) predicts that lagged employment, through its effect on membership, should contain information about wage setting in future periods, the failure of most countries to reject $A_{12}(L) = 0$ constitutes evidence against the membership hysteresis hypothesis.[18]

3.3 Employment Hysteresis in the Federal Republic of Germany: Evidence from Union Membership Data

The Federal Republic of Germany is often regarded as having an institutional structure of collective bargaining conducive to membership hysteresis: powerful industrial unions negotiate at the regional level without a „social contract" of accountability to outsiders, while agreements are regularly extended to cover nonunionized

---

[17] Austrian wage data was taken from Grubb (1984) and is hourly wages rather than weekly earnings.

[18] It should be noted, however, that in the unlikely case that both $\lambda = 1$ and $\rho = 1$, the test will have no power against the membership effect.

enterprises.[19] In this section we examine this economy more closely, employing time series of actual aggregate and disaggregated union membership obtained from the Institut der Deutschen Wirtschaft.[20] To the extent that these data proxy for what we have labeled „membership", our model yields two testable implications.

Table 3. Augmented Dickey-Fuller tests for a unit root in AR representations of DGB Constituent Union Membership 1952–1985*

Union (membership in 000s, yearend 1985)	Values of τ for $p = 0$:
Deutscher Gewerkschaftsbund (DGB) (umbrella organization) (7719)	–2.01
IG Metall (IGM) (metal, automotive workers) (2553)	–1.27
Nahrung-Genuß-Gaststätte (NGG) (food, hotels, restaurants) (267)	–1.34
Bau, Steine, Erden (BSE) (construction, quarrying) (508)	–2.65
IG Chemie (IGC) (chemicals) (650)	–2.18
IG Druck (IGD) (printing trades) (141)	–1.89
IG Bergbau und Energie (IGBE) (mining and energy) (357)	–0.46
Handel, Banken und Versicherungen (HBV) (trade/financial) (371)	–3.31
Gewerkschaft Holz und Kunststoff (GHK) (wood and plastics) (145)	–1.61
Gewerkschaft Textil-Bekleidung (GTB) (clothing, textiles) (259)	–2.41

* τ is defined as in Table 1.

* and ** denote significance at the 5% and 1% level respectively. Critical values for two-sided test from Fuller (1976, Table 8.5.2) 10%: (–3.00,0.0); 5%: (–3.33,0.34); 1%: (–3.75, 0.72).

[19] See Flanagan, et.al. (1983), Soltwedel (1987) and Burda and Sachs (1988).
[20] I thank Mr. Wolfgang Pege for supplying me with these data.

Table 4. Wage equation of bivariate VAR of consumption wages and DGB union membership Federal Republic of Germany (1955–85)
(t-statistics in parenthesis)

	First differences		Levels with time trend	
	$k = 3$	$k = 4$	$k = 3$	$k = 4$
Δw_{t-1}	0.562	0.592	1.27	1.26
	(2.5)	(2.7)	(5.5)	(5.4)
Δw_{t-2}	0.120	0.061	–0.387	-0.333
	(0.5)	(0.3)	(–1.2)	(–0.9)
Δw_{t-3}	0.005	–0.070	0.123	0.185
	(0.0)	(–0.3)	(0.5)	(–0.6)
Δw_{t-4}	–	0.321		0.347
		(1.5)		(1.5)
Δm_{t-1}	–0.793	–0.791	–0.720	–0.683
	(–2.0)	(–2.0)	(–1.8)	(–1.8)
Δm_{t-2}	0.113	0.101	0.603	0.625
	(0.3)	(0.2)	(1.0)	(1.0)
Δm_{t-3}	–0.274	–0.403	–0.350	–0.415
	(–0.6)	(–0.9)	(–0.8)	(0.7)
Δm_{t-4}	–	–0.038	–	–0.019
		(0.2)		(0.0)
TIME	–	–	0.002	–0.002
			(0,5)	(–0.2)
d.w.	1.93	2.04	2.03	1.98
$Q(8)$	6.77	4.81	8.93	6.33
F-statistic*	1.62	1.39	2.73	2.07

* Of the null hypothesis that all coefficients on lagged m are zero in a kth order vector autoregression. Constants are not reported in these regressions.

First, it is trivial to show that if unit roots are induced in the AR representation of employment, and if membership is a distributed lag of employment with a unit root, then membership itself will also contain a unit root in its AR representation. Long time series of union membership are available for the constituent member unions of the West German umbrella organization, the DGB (Deutscher Gewerkschaftsbund). In Table 3 we report Dickey-Fuller tests for unit roots in univariate representations of these time series along the lines of Table 1. We cannot reject unit roots for seven of nine unions considered or for total DGB membership using the critical value of –2.5 ; at the 5% significance level, the null is accepted for all unions examined.

Table 5. „Semistructural" wage equations estimates, Federal Republic of Germany, 1953–1985*

Estimated coefficients						Statistics		
const.	w_{t-1}	ℓ_{t-1}	m_{t-1}	TIME	R^2	s.e.	dw	$Q(8)$
First differences								
0.026	0.522	0.097	–0.699	–	0.30	0.025	1.71	7.12
(2.7)	(2.5)	(0.5)	(–2.0)					
Levels with time trend								
4.35	1.039	–0.012	–0.503	0.001	0.998	0.022	1.96	6.08
(2.0)	(12.7)	(–0.2)	(–0.3)	(0.4)				

Second, the model we derive implies a negative relationship between membership and real wages; all things equal, a larger union will pursue more moderate wage policies.[21] This is also implied in previous work on insider/outsider models by Blanchard and Summers (1986) and Gottfries and Horn (1987). We tested the predictive content of lagged union membership with respect to consumption wages for West Germany, using the time series of total DGB membership for the former. The results are presented in Table 4. While the F-statistic corresponding to the null of irrelevance of membership in wage determination is not significant at the 5% level in any of the four equations, some individual coefficients on lagged membership are significant with the expected sign.

In order to check that the VAR results above are consistent with the interpretation adduced in the text, we estimated a „semi-structural" counterpart to the vector autoregressions above. Rewrite (23) as

$$w_t = \rho w_{t-1} + (\rho / \eta)\ell_{t-1} - (1/\eta)m_{t-1} + \Phi + \xi_t \ . \tag{25}$$

[21] According to (23) this relationship will only evolve over time, since once-lagged employment can actually have a positive sign in a regression if $\rho > \lambda$.

Equation (25) was estimated in both levels and first differences of log consumption wages. Table 5 displays the results. Since the aggregate union membership probably measures the relevant concept for manufacturing with error, the restriction across the coefficients on lagged w, ℓ, and m was not imposed.[22] On the other hand we could not reject this restriction in the first difference equation (likelihood ratio test: $\chi^2(1) = 0.708$), with nonlinear least squares yielding reasonable estimates of 0.382 for ρ and 1.840 for η. The results corroborate the vector autoregression results presented in Table 4: one cannot reject the presence of „membership effects" on wage determination in aggregate West German manufacturing data. The first difference equation implies a short run elasticity of real wages to DGB (union) membership of about –0.7%, with an implicit long-run value well in excess of unity.

4 Conclusions

This investigation was motivated by the view that increases in unemployment in Europe over the past two decades are attributable to divergences of interests of different groups that cannot be mediated by the marketplace. Central to this thesis is the role played by collective bargaining in wage determination as well as the divergence in the interest of unions, whose membership is comprised of currently or recently employed workers, from the those of the unemployed. Models exploiting this idea are capable of translating temporary shocks into permanent or low frequency movements of employment. For a given labor supply, these models provide a ready explanation of the apparent „state dependence" in European unemployment rates.

Empirically, however, this model receives only weak support from European data. We tested some relatively weak implications of the membership hysteresis hypothesis using Dickey-Fuller unit root and Granger causality tests on European labor market data. While these tests derive directly from the model and thus have economic content, they do not require explicit parameter estimation. In general the results were not encouraging in distinguishing high and low unemployment economies.[23] Naturally, our tests have nothing to say about other forms of hysteresis, such as those associated with human or physical capital deterioration.

---

[22] We tried instrumenting m with once lagged values, a procedure that is only appropriate if the measurement error is serially uncorrelated. The results were not very different from the OLS results reported.

[23] Using a large set of sectoral data from fourteen OECD countries, Coe (1989) concludes that hysteresis effects are just as important in the US and Japan as in European countries. Under this

We do find strong evidence of membership hysteresis in the Federal Republic of Germany. Additional tests involving union membership time series offer evidence that the distinction „insiders“ versus „outsiders“ may have empirical content in this economy. The results for Germany are consistent with the institutional features of collective bargaining, in which wage contract provisions are regularly extended to uncovered employees in the same sectors. Industrial unions enjoy a high level of official legitimacy, yet at the same time assume a much less „corporatist“ posture than, say, their Scandinavian counterparts.[24]

References

Abraham K, Medoff J (1985) „Length of Service and Layoffs in Union and Nonunion Groups“. Industrial and Labor Relations Review 38:87–97

Blair D, Crawford D (1984) „Trade Union Preferences and Collective Bargaining“. Quarterly Journal of Economics 99:547–566

Blanchard O, Summers L (1986) „Hysteresis and the European Unemployment Problem“. NBER Macroeconomics Annual 1:15–78

Blythe C (1979) „The Interactions between Collective Bargaining and Government Policies in Selected Member Countries“. In Collective Bargaining and Government Policies, Paris: OECD

Bruno M, Sachs J (1985) The Economics of Worldwide Stagflation. Cambridge: Harvard University Press

Burda M (1987) Essays on the Rise of Unemployment in Europe. PhD dissertation Harvard University

Burda M (1990) Membership, Seniority, and Wage Setting in Democratic Labor Unions“. forthcoming Economica

Burda M, Sachs J (1988) „Assessing High Unemployment in the Federal Republic of Germany“. World Economy

Coe D (1989) „Insider-Outsider Influences on Industry Wages: Evidence from Fourteen Industrialized Countries“. mimeo

Farber H (1986) „The Analysis of Union Behavior“, Chapter 18 in Ashenfelter and Layard, eds., Handbook of Labor Economics. Amsterdam: North-Holland

Faxén K (1982) „Incomes Policy and Centralized Wage Formation“. In A. Boltho, ed., The European Economy: Growth and Crisis. Oxford: Oxford University Press: 365–389.

Flanagan R, Soskice D, Ullman L (1983) Unionism, Economic Stability and Incomes Policies: the European Experience. Washington: Brookings Institution

Fuller W (1976) Introduction to Statistical Time Series. New York: John Wiley and Sons

Geary P, Kennan J (1982) „The Employment-Real Wage Relationship: An International Study“. Journal of Political Economy 90:854–871

---

hypothesis, differing unemployment experiences must be explained by different realizations of aggregate demand (viz., ξ_t) and supply (viz., ν_t) shocks.

[24] Burda and Sachs (1988) and Soltwedel (1987) discuss some of the institutional details of collective bargaining in the Federal Republic of Germany.

Gordon R (1977) „World Inflation and Monetary Accomodation in Eight Countries“. Brookings Papers on Economic Activity 2:409–468

Gordon R (1982) „Why US Wage and Employment Behavior Differs from that in Britain and Japan“. Economic Journal 92:13–44.

Gottfries N, Horn H (1987) „Wage Formation and the Persistence of Unemployment“. Economic Journal 97: 877–886

Grossman G (1983) „Union Wages, Seniority, and Unemployment“. American Economic Review 73:277–290.

Grubb D (1984) „The OECD Data Set“. LSE Centre for Labour Economics Working Paper no 615

Lindbeck A, Snower D (1984) „Involuntary Unemployment as an Insider-Outsider Dilemma“. Seminar Paper No. 282, Institute of International Economic Studies, University of Stockholm

McDonald I, Solow R (1981) „Wage Bargaining and Employment“. American Economic Review 71:896–908

Nelson C, Plosser C (1982) „Trends and Random Walks in Macroeconomic Time Series“. Journal of Monetary Economics 10: 139–162

Oswald A (1982),, The Microeconomic Theory of the Trade Union“. Economic Journal 92:576–595

Oswald A (1984) „Efficient Contracts are on the Labour Demand Curve: Theory and Facts“. mimeo, Princeton Unversity

Oswald A,Turnbull P (1985) „Pay and Employment Determination in Britain: What are Labor Contracts Really Like?“ Oxford Review of Economic Policy 1:80–97

Perry G (1975) „The Determinants of Wage Inflation around the World“. Brookings Papers on Economic Activity 2:403–435

Poterba J, Summers J (1988) „Mean Reversion in Stock Prices: Evidence and Implications“. Journal of Financial Economics 22: 27–59

Sachs J (1979) „Wages, Profits and Macroeconomic Adjustment: A Comparative Study“. Brookings Papers on Economic Activity 2:269–319

Sen A (1970) Collective Choice and Social Welfare. San Francisco: Holden

Simons H (1944) „Some Reflections on Syndicalism“. Journal of Political Economy 52:1–25

Solow R (1985) „Insiders and Outsiders in Wage Determination“. Scandinavian Journal of Economics 87:411–428

Soltwedel R (1984) „Staatliche Interventionen am Arbeitsmarkt: Eine Kritik“. Doctoral dissertation, Christian-Albrecht-Universität zu Kiel

Soltwedel R (1987) „Employment Problems in West Germany – The Role of Institutions, Labor Law and Government Intervention“. Paper presented to the Carnegie-Rochester Conference on Public Policy

Spitäller E „Semi-Annual Wage Equations for the Manufacturing Sector in Six Major Industrial Countries“. Weltwitschaftliches Archiv 112: 300–337

Insider-Outsider Influences on Industry Wages

Evidence from Fourteen Industrialized Countries

By D. T. Coe[1]

Abstract: The persistence of high rates of unemployment in Europe has focused renewed attention on the wage determination process. One aspect which has received particular attention recently is the extent to which wages are determined by insiders, with outsiders having little impact on the wage bargain. If outsiders are disenfranchised in the wage determination process, they may be unable to underbid themselves into employment. The insider-outsider model, and the associated implication of hysteresis, thus provides a possible explanation for persistent involuntary unemployment.

Most empirical work on the importance of the insider-outsider model and hysteresis has been done at the aggregate level, either by testing whether wage growth is related to the level or the change in unemployment, or by testing if employment or unemployment follows a random walk. This paper extends both of these lines of analysis to the industry level. Based on a specification which nests alternative models of the wage determination process, estimation results are presented for fifteen industries using annual data for fourteen industrialized countries, and for pooled time-series cross-country data. The paper also tests the hypothesis that only industry-specific variables are important to the determination of industry wages and considers whether differences in industry wage determination might help to understand cross-country differences in unemployment.

The results offer considerable support to the insider view of wage determination. Industries in which wages seem to be determined by a natural rate/Phillips curve model – the primary competing model considered in the paper – appear to be the exception rather than the rule. Moreover, at the industry level hysteresis does not appear to characterise wage formation in the high-unemployment European countries to a greater extent than in North America and Japan.

[1] David T. Coe, International Monetary-Fund, Research Department, Room 9-309, 700 19th St., N.W. Washington, D.C. 20431, USA.

This paper was started when the author was at the Economics and Statistics Department of the Organisation for Economic Cooperation and Development. Views expressed are the author's and do not necessarily reflect those of either Organisation. I am grateful to Palle Schelde-Andersen, John Martin, Steven Fries and Steve Englander for helpful comments and suggestions; and to Valerie Barca for excellent trans-Atlantic research assistance.

1 Introduction

The persistence of high rates of unemployment in Europe has focused renewed attention on the wage determination process. One aspect which has received particular attention recently is the extent to which wages are determined by insiders – those already employed – with outsiders – the unemployed – having little impact on the wage bargain.[2] If insiders have sufficient market power, because of the costs to the firm of labor turnover, for example, outsiders may be unable to underbid themselves into employment. The basic assumption is that the outsiders are disenfranchised in the wage determination process and the insiders are mainly concerned with their own wages and job security. The insider-outsider model thus provides a possible explanation for persistent involuntary un-employment.[3]

Blanchard and Summers (1988) show that the insider-outsider model will be characterised by hysteresis, in which case there is not a unique natural rate of unemployment. Most empirical work on the importance of hysteresis has been done at the aggregate level, either by testing whether weage growth is related to the level or the change in unemployment, or by testing if employment or unemployment follows a random walk. This paper extends both of these lines of analysis to the industry level.[4]

Compared to aggregate data, industry level data may be better able to discriminate empirically between alternative models of wage determination. The evidence presented here is based on a specification of an industry wage equation which nests a natural rate/Phillips curve model and two versions of the insider-outsider model. Estimated equations are presented for fifteen industries based on annual data for fourteen industrialized countries and based on pooled time-series cross-country data.

---

[2] The insider and outsider groups may, of course, be more broadly defined than the employed and unemployed. See Lindbeck and Snower (1986a, 1988a, 1988b), Solow (1985), Blanchard and Summers (1988), and the references cited therein. In a related paper, Salop (1979) presents a model which makes a central distinction between the internal market for experienced trained workers and the external market for new employees; because the firm is constrained to pay an identical wage, both markets are unable to clear and the result is involuntary unemployment.

[3] Efficiency wage theories are a related, complementary class of models in which firms (rather than insiders) have market power and pay a premium to insiders in order to improve productivity, reduce trunover costs, etc. See Katz (1986) and Lindbeck and Snower (1986b).

[4] Evidence of the importance of hysteresis using aggregate data is presented in Blanchard and Summers (1988), Coe (1988), other papers in Section V of Cross (1988), and in Gordon (1988). A number of recent papers, Nickell and Wadhwani (1988), Nickell and Kong (1988) and Blanchflower, Oswald and Garrett (1987), present evidence of the importance of insider and outsider effects on wages in British establishments using pooled time-series cross-section or cross-section data.

One implication of the insider-outsider model is that wages will be primarily, although not exclusively, determined by conditions specific to individual firms or industries rather than by conditions in the labor market as a whole (Snower, 1988). This paper provides some evidence on this implication of the insider-outsider model by testing the hypothesis that only industry-specific variables are important to the determination of industry wages. The paper also considers whether differences in industry wage determination might help to understand differences in unemployment between high-unemployment European countries and the low-unemployment Nordic and non-European countries.

The following section briefly discusses the data used in the paper and analyses the time-series properties of industry employment data. Section 3 discusses the specification of the wage equation and estimation results are presented in Section 5. The final section is a summary.

2 Data Sources and the Time-Series Properties of Industry Employment

All data are from the recently established OECD sectoral database which is documented in Meyer-zu-Schlochtern (1988). This database contains annual data for the United States, Japan, Germany, France, the United Kingdom, Italy, Canada, Australia, Belgium, Denmark, Finland, the Netherlands, Norway and Sweden. Almost all data are available from at least 1971 to the mid-1980s and many of the data series start from the early 1960s.

The analysis in done for the total manufacturing and service sectors (denoted as TOTAL in Table 1) and for fifteen industries. The manufacturing industries are: food and kindred products (FOOD); textile and leather (TEX); paper and allied products, printing and publication (PAPER); chemicals and allied products, petroleum and coal products, rubber and miscellaneous plastic products (CHEM); primary metals (PRM); machinery and equipment (M&Q); and miscellaneous manufacturing industries (OTHER). The service industries are: wholesale and retail trade, restaurants and hotels (TRAD); transport, storage and communication (TRAN); financial institu-tions, insurance, real estate and business services (FIRE); and community, social and personal services (CS&P). Other industries are mining (MIN), construction (CON), agriculture (AGR) and producers of government services (GOVT).[5]

[5] Data are not available for munufacturing industries in Australia. The sectoral database also includes data for the wood and lumber, clay and glass, and utilities industries.

As Blanchard and Summers (1988) note, one of the implications of the insider-outsider model is that employment will tend to follow a random walk in the presence of shocks. This is because a shock will affect the size of the insider group, and the new insider group will set the wage so as to maintain the new level of employment.

Table 1 reports the Durbin-Watson test for a unit root of Sargan and Bhargava (1983) using annual data for the logarithm of employment.[6] The null hypothesis of a random walk is only rejected for the textile industry in Canada and for the paper and chemical industries in Sweden and Australia; the test statistic is marginally below the 95 per cent confidence level for the manufacturing sector for the United States. If the adjusted Dickey-fuller test is used, the null hypothesis of a random walk can not be rejected for any of the industries in Table 1.

Applying the Durbin-Watson test of Sargan and Bhargava and the adjusted Dickey-Fuller test to annual data from 1963 to 1986 for the logarithm of employment for the remaining ten OECD contries (Austria, Greece, Ireland, Iceland, Luxemburg, New Zealand, Portugal, Spain, Switzerland and Turkey) also gives the result that the null hypothesis of a random walk can not be rejected. This is true for total employment in all countries as well as for employment in the industrial and service sectors and in agriculture.[7]

The power of these unit root tests may not be great; and failure to reject does not imply the truth of the unit-root null hypothesis. Nevertheless, the extent to which employment developments in virtually all industries and sectors and for all OECD countries are not inconsistent with a random walk is impressive. This evidence of a high degree of persistence in employment is consistent with one of the key implications of the insider-outsider model – the best predictor of employment in one period is employment in the previous period.[8]

---

[6] In most cases, the sample period for the unit root tests is from the early 1960s to 1986. For the United States, Japan, the United Kingdom (services), Canada (services), Denmark, Sweden, Australia and the Netherlands, the sample period is from the late 1960s or early 1970s to 1986.

[7] The same results are also obtained for total employment for the countries reported in Table 1, confirming and extending results reported by Blanchard and Summers (1988) for aggregate unemployment in the United States and the United Kingdom. Unreported results discussed in this and subsequent sections are available from the author.

[8] When the Sargan-Bhargava or the adjusted Dickey-Fuller tests are applied to the other variables used in the empirical analysis which follows, the null hypothesis of a unit root can not be rejected for the annual data for the logarithm of aggregate and industry compensation per employee, industry output prices, aggregate unemployment rates or aggregate consumption prices. When applied to the logarithm of industry labor productivity, the hypothesis of a unit root is rejected only for U.S. primary metals, Germany other manufacturing and mining, U.K. other manufacturing, Canada paper and chemicals, Denmark transportation, and Australia FIRE. Thus, since virtually all of the data are integrated of first order, a necessary condition for the existence of an equilibrium relationship between the variables is met (cf. Hendry, 1986).

Table 1. Sargan and Bhargava test for a unit root (Durbin-Watson test on the logarithm of employment)

		Manufacturing Industries						
	TOTAL	FOOD	TEX	PAPER	CHEM	PRM	M&E	OTHER
United States	1.061	0.158	0.181	0.110	0.370	0.176	0.795	0.498
Japan	0.492	0.446	0.100	0.426	0.284	0.138	0.314	0.954
Germany	0.101	0.066	0.025	0.058	0.157	0.050	0.384	0.120
France	0.128	0.265	0.026	0.104	0.044	0.087	0.199	0.341
U.K.	0.065	0.064	0.038	0.076	0.147	0.056	0.069	0.114
Italy	0.158	0.220	0.111	0.149	0.074	0.171	0.068	0.069
Canada	0.627	0.085	1.105*	0.072	0.069	0.411	0.141	0.177
Australia	0.295	0.408	0.225	1.988**	1.347*	0.488	0.298	0.563
Belgium	0.041	0.024	0.025	0.061	0.153	0.072	0.100	0.086
Denmark	0.229	0.119	0.054	0.217	0.434	0.179	0.655	0.449
Finland	0.071	0.080	0.156	0.052	0.033	0.046	0.044	0.612
Netherlands	0.052	0.047	0.040	0.159	0.248	0.148	0.070	0.472
Norway	0.144	0.495	0.029	0.290	0.201	0.185	0.106	0.082
Sweden	0.125	0.178	0.048	1.277*	1.190*	0.089	0.274	0.113

	Service Industries					Other Industries			
	TOTAL	TRAD	TRAN	FIRE	CS&P	MIN	CON	AGR	GOVT
United Sates	0.055	0.047	0.140	0.039	0.035	0.134	0.250	0.447	0.052
Japan	0.049	0.056	0.502	0.045	0.051	0.133	0.142	0.060	0.074
Germany	0.118	0.174	0.387	0.025	0.024	0.039	0.135	0.017	0.021
France	0.064	0.023	0.086	0.075	0.019	n. a.	0.121	0.019	0.065
U.K.	0.085	0.168	0.197	0.053	0.066	0.138	0.594	0.078	0.030
Italy	n. a.	0.032	0.026	n.a.	0.049	n. a.	0.133	0.029	0.020
Australia	0.066	0.176	0.151	0.068	0.056	0.456	0.677	0.866	n.a.
Canada	0.065	0.070	0.169	0.055	0.086	0.191	0.310	0.107	0.082
Belgium	0.066	0.380	0.351	0.037	0.049	n. a.	0.111	0.021	0.062
Denmark	0.152	0.105	0.085	0.041	0.485	0.371	0.164	0.039	0.035
Finland	0.136	0.075	0.072	0.024	0.073	0.184	0.324	0.021	0.017
Netherlands	0.087	0.458	0.454	0.056	0.056	0.296	0.126	0.052	0.048
Norway	0.078	0.047	0.252	0.034	0.031	0.035	0.136	0.023	0.019
Sweden	0.079	0.754	0.102	0.070	0.533	0.110	0.100	0.082	0.049

* indicates rejects null hypothesis of a random walk at 95 percent confidence level (critical value 1.069).

** indicates rejects null hypothesis of a random walk at 99 percent confidence level (critical value 1.470).

Note: The figures are Durbin-Watson statistics from the regression ln (employment) = constant + error.

3 Equation Specification

Nickell and Wadhwani (1988) have examined the importance of insider influences in wage determination based on a "union model with insiders" in which wages are bargained for *ex-ante* but prices, output and employment are set *ex-post* by the firm. In the bargaining process the unions only consider the welfare of existing workers, i.e. the insiders. In this model, the insider forces operating on a firm's wages are the firm's output price, employment and productivity, a measure of union power faced by the firm and a measure of the firm's liquidity; the outsider forces are aggregate wages, consumer prices, the aggregate unemployment rate and unemployment benefits.

The following specification for the industry wage equations nests alternative models of the wage formation process and incorporates many of the same explanatory variables as in Nickell and Wadhwani (1988):

$$\begin{aligned} \Delta \ln(W_i / P_i) &= \alpha_1 \Delta \ln E_i + a_2 \Delta \ln Q_i + \alpha_3 \ln\{W_i / P_i) / Q_i\}_{t-1} \\ &\quad + \beta_1 \Delta \ln(P_i / P) + \beta_2 1nU + \text{constant} + \text{error} \end{aligned}$$

where Δ is the first difference operator and 1n indicates natural logarithms. W_i is compensation per employee in industry i;[9] P_i is the implicit output deflator for industry i; E_i is employment in industry i; Q_i is labor productivity (real value-added output per employee) in industry i; P is the aggregate implicit deflator for private consumption expenditures; and U is the aggregate unemployment rate.

The equation states that the growth of real product wages in each industry is related to a number of industry-specific variables – the growth of industry output prices, employment, and productivity and an error-correction term – to consumr price inflation, and to the logarithm of the aggregate unemployment rate.[10] In the short run, the specification allows nominal wage growth in an industry to be related to only the growth of the industry's output price ($\beta_1 = 0$), to only the growth of economy-wide consumer prices ($\beta_1 = -1$), or to a weighted average of the two ($-1 < \beta_1 < 0$). In the long run, the error correction specification imposes homogeneity between the levels of the real product wage and productivity in each industry. Expected signs are a_1, $a_2 > 0$ and a_3, β_1, $\beta_2 < 0$.

---

[9] It is implicitly assumed that bargaining is for total compensation including non-wage labor costs (employers' contributions for social security and pensions), rather than just earnings. Compensation per employee will be influenced by changes in hours and the demographic/human capital mix of the work force. The impact on wages of changes in these variables will be captured, to some extent, by the productivity and relative wage terms.

[10] The logarithm of the unemployment rate is, in terms of linearity, intermediate between a level and reciprocal specification.

The alternative models of the wage formation process which are nested in the above specification are the natural rate/Phillips curve model, an insider-outsider/hysteresis model, and a real-wage bargaining model which shares some of the long-run properties of the insider-outsider model. The fundamental differences between the alternative models concern the nature of the long-run equilibrium and the forces which drive the labor market to that equilibrium. The key estimated coefficients which discriminate between the alternative models are those for the aggregate unemployment rate (β_2), the change in industry employment (α_1) and the error-correction term, the latter determining if the equation is in level ($\alpha_3 < 0$) or growth rate form ($\alpha_3 = 0$):

i. The *natural rate/Phillips curve model* is implied if the estimated equation is in growth-rate form ($\alpha_3 = 0$) and the level of unemployment exerts a significant negative effect ($\beta_2 < 0$). In long-run equilibrium, unemployment is at the natural rate and real wage growth is equal to the growth of trend productivity. It is the gap between the actual and the natural rate of unemployment for the economy as a whole which is the main factor driving the labor market to equilibrium.[11] If the change in industry employment, an insider variable, is significant ($\alpha_1 > 0$), this would imply loops around the Phillips curve à la Lipsey.
ii. The *insider-outsider/hysteresis model* is implied if the estimated equation is in growth-rate form ($\alpha_3 = 0$) and changes in industry employment have a significant effect on wage growth ($\alpha_1 > 0$) but the level of unemployment does not ($\beta_2 = 0$). Like the Phillips curve model, real wages grow at the same rate as trend productivity in long-run equilibrium. But here, since unemployment is not significant, it is the growth of industry employment, an insider variable, which is the driving force to labormarket equilibriuj.[12]

---

[11] In the case where $\alpha_3 = 0$, the estimated equation becomes:

$$\Delta \ln(W_i/P_i) = \alpha_0 + \alpha_1 \Delta \ln E_i + \alpha_2 \Delta \ln Q_i + \beta_1 \Delta \ln(P_i/P) + \beta_2 \ln U,$$
$$\text{with } \alpha_0 = -\beta_2 \ln U^* + (1 - \alpha_2)\Delta \ln Q^* - \alpha_1 \Delta \ln E^*$$

where U^* is the natural rate, $\Delta \ln Q^*$ is trend productivity growth and $\Delta \ln E^*$ is trend labor force growth. In long-run equilibrium $U = U^*$, $\Delta \ln Q_i = \Delta \ln Q^*$, $\Delta \ln E_i = \Delta \ln E^*$ and $\Delta \ln P_i = \Delta \ln P$, and hence the growth of real wages equals the growth of trend productivity. The specification only includes contemporaneous variables which, except for the United States and Canada, is consistent with the predominance of annual bargaining cycles and widespread indexation.

[12] Thus the term "hysteresis" is used somewhat loosely to refer to a model in which wage growth is only affected by the change in employment. Note that there could still be a unique natural rate if price inflation is sensitive to the gap between actual and potential output and if there is a unique relationship (via Okun's law) between the output gap and the labor market gap. The estimated equations can not discriminate between a situation where the natural rate increases due to hystere-

iii. The *real-wage bargaining model* is implied if the estimated equation is in level form ($\alpha_3 = 0$) indicating a long-run equilibrium relationship between the *level* of real wages and the *level* of productivity.[13] The primary equilibrating force here is the insiders' real-wage target which is represented by the error-correction term. If unemployment has a significant impact ($\beta_2 = 0$), there is a long-run relationship between the level of wages and the level of unemployment; this implies a long-run relationship between the growth of wages and the change in unemployment similar to the insider-outsider/hysteresis model. In this case, the level of unemployment may affect wage growth in the short run (the mean lag is $-(1+\alpha_3)/\alpha_3$), but in the long run wage growth is only affected by changes in the unemployment rate.[14]

To illustrate the differences between these alternative models, consider a shock which temporarily reduces the growth of employment in all industries, implying a corresponding increase in the aggregate unemployment rate. This higher unemployment rate will persist after the growth of employment returns to its preshock level and then remains constant. In the natural rate/Phillips curve model, there is downward pressure on wage growth which, as it gets incorporated into inflation expectations, remaines so long as aggregate unemployment is in excess of the natural rate.[15] The wage disinflation process will increase employment through factor substitution and increased profitability on the supply side as real wages fall, as well as through real-balance effects on the demand side as inflation declines in the context of stable growth of nominal government expenditures and money. This dynamic equilibrating process will continue until the labor market is in equilibrium at the natural rate of unemployment.

In the insider-outsider/hysteresis model, however, the temporary decline in employment growth would have only a temporary impact on the growth of wages,

---

sis-type effects as opposed to changes in its structural determinants. Since the late 1970s, however, it is difficult to identify structural changes which would have contributed to large increases in the natural rate (cf. Chan-Lee *et al.*, 1987).

[13] The basic references are Sargan (1964) and Kuh (1967).

[14] Based on the general specification given in the text, the underlying levels equation can be written as:

$$\ln W_i = \alpha_0 + \alpha_1 \Delta \ln E_i + \alpha_2 \ln Q_i - (\alpha_2 + \alpha_3)\ln Q_{it-1} + (1+\alpha_3)\ln W_{it-1}$$
$$+ (1+\beta_1)\ln P_1 - (1+\beta_1 + \alpha_3)\ln P_{it-1} - \beta_1 \Delta \ln P + \beta_2 \ln U.$$

If $\alpha_3 > 0$ the equation has unstable dynamic properties. In long-run equilibrium, and denoting the steady-state growth of productivity as k_Q and similarly for inflation (k_p) and the growth of the labor force (k_E), the equation becomes: $\ln(W_i/P_i) = \ln Q_i - (\beta_2/\alpha_3)\ln U + A_0$, where $A_0 = -(1/\alpha_3)\,[\alpha_0 + \alpha_1 k_E + \alpha_1 k_Q + k_P]$.

[15] That is, the short-run Phillips curves continually shift downward. This is simply the mirror-image of Friedman's (1968) accelerationist hypothesis.

eventhough the unemployment rate remained at a higher level. In effect, wage growth would be moderated as some of the insiders lost their jobs, but thereafter wage growth would be geared to maintaining employment constant at its new level, i.e., wage growth would be unaffected by the fact that there was now a larger pool of the unemployed. Similarly in the real-wage bargaining model, the target level of real wages may be affected by the higher unemployment, but not the growth of wages. Thus, in either the insider-outsider/hysteresis or the real-wage bargaining models, unlike the Phillips curve model, there is no ongoing impact on wage growth which would tend over time to reduce unemployment to its natural rate.

These alternative models are very similar to the aggregate models of wage determination discussed by Nickell (1988) and Andersen (1989), although specifying them as industry equations allows a sharper distinction between insider and outsider influences on wage formation. As Nickell notes, there are strong differences between the alternative models,[16] but discriminating between them is an empirical matter.

4 Empirical Results

A. Individual Country Wage Equations

Table 2 summarzies the evidence for the alternative models of wage determination based on estimated wage equations for 196 industries:[17] industries where the estimation results support the natural rate/Phillips curve model are denoted N, the insider-outsider/hysteresis model are denoted H, and the real-wage bargaining model are denoted R. In about 70 per cent of the industries where the relevant coefficient estimates are significant and correctly signed, wage formation appears to be dominated by insiders, either because the estimated equation is characterised by hysteresis or by insiders bargaining for a target real wage. In most of these industries, the estimated coefficients on the unemployment rate are not significantly different from zero. In those industries where the unemployment rate is insignifi-

---

[16] In particular the two insider-outsider models can only reveal the long-run equilibrium level of unemployment when combined with the remaining supply-side equations, whereas the natural-rate/Phillips curve model pins down the long-run equilibrium rate of unemployment by looking only at wage-bargaining behaviour.

[17] All equations were tested for a break in 1980. The hypothesis of temporal stability was rejected at the 5 per cent confidence level for the U.S. chemicals, primary metals, service sector, transportation; Japan paper, service sector; Germany primary metals; U.K. mining; Canada chemicals; Australia manufacturing sector, FIRE, mining; Belgium government; Denmark trade; Finland construction; Norway paper, government; Sweden transportation, FIRE, agriculture.

cant, the relative inflation and industry-specific variables are generally significant explain a high proportion of industry wage developments.[18]

The estimated coefficients on the relative inflation term are generally highly significant and often close to minus one, indicating that industry wages are more closely indexed to aggregate consumption prices than they are to industry output prices. This is not inconsistent with the insider-outsider view of wage determination since the real consumption wage (W_i/P) as well as the real product wage (W_i/P_i)will be important to insiders. The aggregate variable which is better able to discriminate between the alternative models is the unemployment rate representing conditions in the labor market as a whole. As noted, the unemployment rate dos not appear to exert an important influence on wage growth in most industries.

The estimated equations are consistent with the natural rate/Phillips curve model in slightly less than 25 per cent of the industries in Table 2. It is noteworthy that the natural rate model does not appear to be more relevant to the formation of industry wages in the United States and Japan compared to the high-unemployment European countries.

Table 2. Nested tests for alternative models of wage formation
N indicates a natural rate/Phillips curve model; H indicates an insider-outsider/hysteresis model; R indicates a real-wage bargaining model

	Manufacturing industries						
	food	textiles	paper	chem	pr. metals	m& equip	other
U.S.	R	R	H	R	H	H	H
Japan	–	R*	N	R*	N	H	R
Germany	N	N	N	H	R*	N	N
France	–	–	R	N	N	N	R
U.K.	R*	N	R*	N	R*	R*	R
Italy	N	R*	–	H	H	H	R*
Canada	H	N	H	N	R	N	H
Belgium	N	H	R*	N	N	N	H
Denmark	–	H	H	N	H	H	R*
Finland	H	N	H	H	H	N	N
Netherlands	R*	H	N	R	R	N	R
Norway	R*	H	R*	H	R*	H	R
Sweden	R*	H	R*	R*	H	R	H

[18] If the significance of the two aggregate variables taken together (inflation, β_1, and the unemployment rate, β_2) is tested, the restriction ($\beta_1 = \beta_2 = 0$) is rejected for most industries in virtually all countries, with the exception of France. In almost all cases, this result reflects the significance of the estimated coefficient on the relative inflation term (β_1) rather than the unemployment rate (β_2).

Table 2. (continued)

	Service industries				Other Industries			
	trade	trans	FIRE	CS&P	mining	const	agric	govt
U.S.	H	H	–	R	R	H	–	H
Japan	H	N	–	–	–	H	–	N
Germaniy	R	N	N	R	R*	N	R*	H
France	R	H	n.a.	–	n.a.	H	–	N
U.K.	H	H	R	H	H	N	R*	H
Italy	–	R	n.a.	–	n.a.	N	N	H
Canada	H	N	R	–	H	H	H	H
Australia	H	H	N	H	R*	H	R*	H
Belgium	N	–	n.a.	–	n.a.	H	–	H
Denmark	N	R	H	H	H	H	–	H
Finland	N	N	N	N	N	N	H	H
Netherlands	N	N	n.a.	R	H	N	–	H
Norway	N	R	–	H	H	R	R	H
Sweden	R*	N	N	R*	R*	R*	R	H

Notes: This table summarises the results of the nested tests for the alternative models, as discussed in the text. In the estimated equations denoted "N", $\alpha_3 = 0$, $\beta_2 < 0$; in those denoted "H", $\alpha_3 = 0$, $\beta_2 = 0$, and $\alpha_1 > 0$; in those denoted "R" $\alpha_3 < 0$; in those denoted "R*", $\alpha_3 < 0$ and $\beta_2 < 0$. "–" indicates that the relevant estimated coefficients are not significantly different from zero and/or perversly signed.

Estimated equations for the manufacturing and service sectors are reported in Table 3. In most cases, the sectoral wage equations are consistent with either an insider-outsider/hysteresis or real-wage bargaining model.[19] The only natural rate equations are for the manufacturing and service sectors in Germany and Finland; for the manufacturing sector in Japan, France and Belgium; and for the service sector in Canada and Australia. The wage-restraining impact of unemployment is greater in the manufacturing than in the service sector in all countries except Germany, Australia and Finland (in Canada the impact is about the same). In 11 of the 26 equations, the estimated coefficients on the unemployment rate are not significantly different from zero and/or perversely signed.

[19] Taken together, the two aggregate variables appear to be more important to the determination of wages in the manufacturing sector – the restriction that $\beta_1 = \beta_2 = 0$ is rejected for all countries except Japan, Italy and Australia – than in the service sector – where the restriction is only rejected for Germany, Australia, Denmark, Norway and Sweden.

Table 3. Wage equations for the manufacturing and service sectors

Estimated equations: $\Delta \ln(W_i / P_i) = \alpha_0 + \alpha_1 \Delta \ln E_i + \alpha_2 \Delta \ln I_i + \alpha_3 \ln((W_i / P_i) / Q_i)_{t-1}$
$+\beta_1 \Delta \ln(P_i / P) + \beta_2 \ln U + \text{error}$

	α_0	α_1	α_2	α_3	β_1	β_2	RBSQ DW	obs model
A. Manufacturing sector								
United States	2.09 (2.5)	0.95 (15)	0.23 (3.3)	−0.13 (2.4)	−0.77 (8.1)	−0.01 (0.6)	0.99 1.84	17 R
Japan	1.56 (1.1)	1.06 (5.3)	0.001 (0.0)	−0.09 (1.0)	−0.27 (1.2)	−0.05 (2.1)	0.87 1.14	15 N
Germany	−0.50 (0.4)	1.58 (8.1)	0.45 (2.8)	0.03 (0.5)	−0.68 (3.7)	−0.01 (2.3)	0.88 2.09	24 N
France	−2.40 (1.3)	−0.54 (0.9)	−0.02 (0.0)	0.17 (1.4)	0.50 (1.1)	−0.09 (3.5)	0.70 2.11	15 N
United Kingdom	4.18 (3.3)	0.12 (0.5)	0.28 (2.2)	−0.26 (3.3)	−0.33 (2.3)	−0.08 (4.4)	0.84 2.28	15 R
Italy	2.64 (3.0)	1.76 (3.9)	0.16 (1.2)	−0.17 (2.8)	−0.04 (0.1)	−0.01 (0.2)	0.78 2.07	25 R
Canada	1.99 (2.9)	0.31 (5.2)	0.43 (7.0)	−0.13 (2.8)	−0.75 (4.5)	−0.06 (6.3)	0.90 2.08	23 R
Australia	0.64 (0.3)	0.98 (2.9)	0.78 (2.6)	−0.04 (0.3)	0.12 (0.3)	−0.03 (1.4)	0.64 2.08	16 H
Belgium	0.28 (0.2)	1.10 (2.0)	0.50 (3.1)	−0.01 (0.1)	−0.82 (3.2)	−0.04 (2.6)	0.85 2.06	15 N
Denmark	−0.13 (0.1)	0.94 (3.8)	0.34 (1.6)	0.01 (0.1)	−0.54 (2.7)	−0.02 (1.1)	0.76 2.28	19 H
Finland	−0.11 (0.2)	1.59 (8.5)	0.09 (0.5)	0.01 (0.3)	−1.16 (8.9)	−0.03 (2.1)	0.86 1.98	25 N
Netherlands	3.47 (2.4)	0.39 (1.0)	0.20 (1.6)	−0.25 (2.3)	−0.87 (5.7)	−0.05 (4.7)	0.90 1.91	16 R
Norway	3.59 (2.9)	0.20 (0.4)	−0.16 (0.7)	−0.28 (2.9)	−0.56 (3.0)	−0.07 (2.1)	0.77 1.40	23 R
Sweden	3.47 (2.3)	0.53 (0.7)	0.28 (0.6)	−0.25 (2.2)	−0.67 (2.6)	−0.13 (2.1)	0.62 1.31	15 R
B. Service sector								
United States	−0.09 (0.2)	0.95 (3.6)	0.85 (2.8)	0.01 (0.2)	−0.62 (1.4)	−0.004 (0.1)	0.81 2.95	15 H

Table 3. (continued)

	α_0	α_1	α_2	α_3	β_1	β_2	RBSQ DW	obs model
Japan	2.97	1.04	0.19	–0.18	–0.55	0.02	0.88	15
	(2.1)	(2.4)	(1.3)	(2.1)	(2.6)	(0.3)	2.27	R
Germany	2.30	1.09	0.41	–0.15	–0.76	–0.02	0.83	15
	(1.1)	(2.0)	(1.5)	(1.1)	(1.7)	(2.8)	2.12	N
France	4.05	0.86	0.23	–0.27	0.01	0.05	0.72	14
	(1.8)	(2.2)	(0.7)	(1.8)	(0.0)	(1.1)	2.28	R/H
United Kingdom	4.36	1.06	0.29	–0.29	–0.59	0.03	0.07	15
	(0.8)	(1.5)	(0.4)	(0.8)	(0.6)	(0.6)	2.00	H
Italy	1.63	0.33	0.32	–0.11	–0.48	0.03	0.57	15
	(1.4)	(0.4)	(1.0)	(1.3)	(1.3)	(0.5)	2.63	–
Canada	0.13	0.64	0.70	0.002	–0.43	–0.07	0.74	14
	(0.1)	(1.8)	(1.9)	(0.0)	(0.9)	(1.8)	2.62	N/H
Australia	–7.02	1.33	1.11	0.50	–0.10	–0.15	0.47	15
	(2.3)	(2.2)	(1.5)	(2.3)	(0.2)	(2.6)	2.21	N
Denmark	8.31	0.20	0.31	–0.65	–0.55	0.02	0.76	15
	(3.9)	(0.6)	(2.0)	(3.9)	(3.7)	(2.2)	2.63	R
Finland	–1.63	1.02	1.25	0.13	–1.77	–0.06	0.68	15
	(0.6)	(2.6)	(1.8)	(0.7)	(2.1)	(2.7)	2.30	N
Norway	3.60	1.52	0.08	–0.28	–1.05	–.003	0.93	15
	(6.8)	(5.0)	(0.3)	(6.8)	(6.6)	(0.2)	2.97	R
Sweden	2.98	1.18	0.34	–0.22	–0.24	–0.37	0.69	15
	(2.0)	(1.4)	(0.9)	(2.0)	(0.7)	(3.7)	1.86	R

Notes: Absolute values of t-statistics are reported in parentheses. ln indicates logarithms, Δ indicates first differences, and subscript i indicates either the manufacturing or service sectors. W_i is compensation per employee, P_i is the implicit output deflator, E_i is employment, Q_i is value-added output per employee, P is the aggregate implicit deflator for private consumption expenditures, U is the aggregate unemployment rate. The alternative models are specified in Table 2. The estimation period is 1969 to 1985 for the United States (*m*anufacturing); 1962 to 1985 for Germany (*m*); 1962 to 1984 for Canada (*m*); 1967 to 1985 for Denmark (*m*); 1963 to 1985 for Norway (*m*); 1961 to 1985 for Italy (*m*) and Finland (*m*); 1970 to 1985 for equations with 16 observations; 197 to 1985 for equations with 15 observations; and 1971 to 1984 for equations with 14 observations.

The results discussed thus far provide considerable support to the insider view of wage determination. Although consumer prices are generally important, high levels of aggregate unemployment appear to have no significant restraining effect on wage growth in most industries. The evidence in favor of the insider-outsider/hysteresis and real-wage bargaining models appears to be somewhat stronger for service industries, and at the industry rather than the sectoral level.

One potential problem with these results is that some of the equations have been estimated on a relatively few number of annual observations. In addition, the aggregation to the sectoral level inevitably blurs the distinction between industry-specific and aggregate variables. Both of these potential problems are avoided in the empirical results reported in the next section.

B. Pooled Time-Series Cross-Country Wage Equations

Tables 4 and 5 report wage equations estimated on pooled time-series cross-country data. Except for the country-specific constants, which would allow natural rates, for example, to differ, wages within each industry are assumed to be determined in a like manner across countries. In Table 4 the results are based on data for all countries; in Table 5 the results are based on data for only the high-unemployment European countries (Germany, France, the U.K., Italy, Belgium, Denmark and the Netherlands).

Table 4. Industry wage equations (pooled time-series cross-country data)

Estimated equations: $\Delta \ln(W_i / P_i) = \alpha_1 \Delta \ln E_i + \alpha_2 \Delta \ln Q_i + \alpha_3 \ln((W_i / P_i) / Q_i)_{t-1}$
$+\beta_1 \Delta \ln(P_i / P) + \beta_2 \ln U$ + (country - specific constants) + error

Industry (i)	α_1	α_2	α_3	β_1	β_2	RBSQ SE	obs model
Manufacturing industries							
Total	0.74 (11)	0.23 (5.0)	–0.14 (4.9)	–0.66 (11)	–0.04 (10)	0.78 0.02	196 R
Food	0.40 (3.4)	0.12 (1.8)	–0.11 (5.4)	–0.93 (21)	–0.03 (7.1)	0.85 0.03	182 R
Textiles	0.81 (14)	0.41 (8.6)	–0.02 (1.0)	–0.55 (8.9)	–0.03 (4.4)	0.77 0.03	182 N
Paper	0.41 (4.1)	0.28 (6.7)	–0.14 (4.7)	–0.79 (22)	–0.04 (7.3)	0.81 0.03	182 R

Table 3. (continued)

Industry (i)	α_1	α_2	α_3	β_1	β_2	RBSQ SE	obs model
Chemicals	0.52	0.12	–0.11	–0.93	–0.02	0.88	182
	(6.9)	(3.9)	(5.4)	(31)	(4.9)	0.03	R
Primary metals	0.84	0.14	–0.07	–0.92	–0.03	0.89	182
	(12)	(5.0)	(3.7)	(33)	(4.5)	0.04	R
Machinery & equip.	0.84	0.38	–0.08	–0.63	–0.03	0.88	182
	(16)	(10)	(3.4)	(13)	(7.2)	0.02	R
Other manufacturing	0.37	0.21	–0.07	–0.81	–0.04	0.87	182
	(5.6)	(5.0)	(4.1)	(14)	(6.0)	0.04	R
Service industries							
Total	0.97	0.36	–0.10	–0.45	–0.01	0.66	196
	(7.7)	(4.2)	(5.9)	(4.9)	(3.8)	0.02	R
Trade	0.95	0.35	–0.09	–0,66	–0.02	0.72	196
	(8.1)	(5.6)	(4.7)	(10)	(4.7)	0.02	R
Transportation	0.75	0.24	–0.14	–0.74	–0.02	0.79	196
	(7.0)	(4.6)	(6.6)	(14)	(5.1)	0.02	R
FIRE	0.82	0.23	–0.04	–0.92	–0.01	0.62	140
	(6.3)	(2.0)	(2.8)	(9.5)	(1.5)	0.03	R
CS & P services	0.79	0.58	–0.06	–0.16	–0.01	0.53	126
	(6.4)	(5.8)	(4.1)	(1.9)	(1.8)	0.03	R
Other industries							
Mining	0.99	0.05	0.01	–1.02	–0.07	0.79	121
	(9.3)	(1.2)	(0.4)	(17)	(3.0)	0.08	N
Construction	1.01	0.36	–0.04	–0.55	–0.02	0.76	196
	(18)	(7.0)	(1.9)	(9.2)	(5.0)	0.03	N/R
Agriculture	0.16	0.12	–0.15	–0.77	–0.02	0.81	196
	(0.9)	(2.6)	(5.5)	(22)	(3.2)	0.04	R
Government	1.04	1.03	0.01	0.03	6E-7	0.95	196
	(35)	(32)	(1.1)	(2.4)	(5E-4)	0.005	H

Notes: Variable definitions are given in the note to Table 3 except that the "i"s refer to in-dustries. The alternative models are specified in Table 2. All equations are estimated by ordinary least squares on pooled annual data from 1971 to 1984 for the United States, Japan, Germany, France, the United Kingdom, Italy, Canada, Australia, Belgium, Denmark, Finland, the Netherlands, Norway and Sweden. Industries with 182 observations do not include data for Australia; FIRE does not include data for France, Italy, Belgium and the Netherlands; Mining is from 1974 to 1984 and does not include data for France, Italy and Belgium.

Table 5. Industry wage equations for high-unemployment European countries (pooled time-series cross country data)

Estimated equations: $\Delta \ln(W_i / P_i) = \alpha_1 \Delta \ln E_i + \alpha_2 \Delta \ln Q_i + \alpha_3 \ln((W_i / P_i) / Q_i)_{t-1}$
$+\beta_1 \Delta \ln(P_i / P) + \beta_2 \ln U +$ (country - specific constants) + error

Industry (i)	α_1	α_2	α_3	β_1	β_2	RBSQ SE	obs model
Eropean manufacturing industries							
Total	0.73	0.24	–0.08	–0.52	–0.03	0.71	98
	(6.0)	(4.0)	(1.8)	(5.3)	(6.3)	0.02	N
Food	0.21	0.07	–0.15	–0.88	–0.03	0.74	98
	(1.0)	(0.5)	(4.1)	(11)	(6.1)	0.03	R
Textiles	1.01	0.34	–0.01	–0.61	–0.03	0.79	98
	(11)	(5.9)	(0.4)	(7.3)	(2.8)	0.03	N
Paper	0.49	0.25	–0.19	–0.64	–0.04	0.64	98
	(3.0)	(3.3)	(2.9)	(7.3)	(5.1)	0.03	R
Chemicals	0.74	0.13	–0.07	–0.85	–0.02	0.84	98
	(6.5)	(3.6)	(2.6)	(16)	(3.7)	0.03	R
Primary metals	0.86	0.21	–0.08	–0.88	–0.03	0.89	98
	(7.8)	(4.5)	(2.7)	(21)	(4.0)	0.04	R
Machinery & equip.	0.89	0.45	–0.06	–6.3	–0.02	0.84	98
	(8.7)	(6.8)	(1.5)	(9.0)	(5.2)	0.02	N
Other manufacture	0.79	0.24	–0.11	–0.79	–0.03	0.82	98
	(5.1)	(3.6)	(3.2)	(10)	(4.5)	0.04	R
European service industries							
Total	1.03	0.28	–0.11	–0.45	–0.01	0.69	98
	(6.0)	(2.8)	(4.9)	(3.9)	(2.5)	0.02	R
Trade	1.07	0.21	–0.09	–0.85	–0.02	0.73	98
	(6.4)	(2.5)	(3.9)	(8.9)	(3.3)	0.02	R
Transportation	1.04	0.36	–0.12	–0.50	–0.01	0.77	98
	(5.9)	(5.6)	(4.0)	(6.6)	(3.0)	0.02	R
FIRE	1.04	–0.01	0.06	–0.87	–0.01	0.56	42
	(4.0)	(0.1)	(1.3)	(5.7)	(1.3)	0.02	H
CS & P services	1.04	0.56	–0.08	–0.07	–.002	0.51	98
	(4.9)	(3.1)	(3.2)	(0.5)	(0.3)	0.03	R

Table 5. (continued)

Industry (i)	α_1	α_2	α_3	β_1	β_2	RBSQ SE	obs model
Other European industries							
Mining	1.18 (6.4)	0.02 (0.3)	0.04 (0.8)	−1.00 (6.5)	−0.07 (1.3)	0.71 0.11	44 H
Construction	1.13 (13)	0.26 (3.5)	−0.01 (0.4)	−0.84 (8.0)	−0.02 (3.4)	0.73 0.03	98 N
Agriculture	−0.25 (0.8)	0.08 (1.1)	−0.15 (3.2)	−0.85 (14)	0.01 (1.3)	0.80 0.04	98 R
Government	1.01 (24)	1.01 (30)	−.002 (0.2)	0.01 (0.6)	−.0005 (0.4)	0.96 0.004	98 H

Notes: See notes to Tables 2, 3 and 4. All equations are estimated by ordinary least squares on pooled annual data from 1971 to 1985 for Germany, France, the United Kingdom, Italy, Belgium, Denmark and the Netherlands. FIRE does not include data for France, Italy, Belgium and the Netherlands; Mining is from 1974 to 1984 and does not include data for France, Italy and Belgium.

As in the individual-country equations, the estimated coefficients on the relative inflation term (β_1) are highly significant, and often near minus one in all industries with the exception of community, social and personal (CS & P) services and government. The estimated coefficients on the unemployment rate are correctly signed and significant in all industries except FIRE, CS & P and government in both country groupings; and also in mining and agriculture in the European countries. Unemployment appears to have a stronger impact on wages in manufacturing than in services, the same result obtained in the previous section.

The most dominant impression from Tables 4 and 5, however, is the preponderance of industries where the estimation results support the real-wage bargaining model. Wage formation appears to be consistent with the natural rate model ($\alpha_3 = 0, \beta_2 < 0$) only in the textile and mining industries in the equations estimated on data from all countries; and in the manufacturing sector, textiles, machinery and equipment, and construction industries for the high-unemployment European countries. For the other industries, the impact of the unemployment rate on the *growth* of wages is either insignificant or temporary, in the latter case because the estimation results imply a long-run level relationship between wages and unemployment ($\alpha_3 < 0$).[20]

[20] The mean lags are quite long, usually from 6 to 12 years.

Table 6 reports tests for differences in wage formation between the high-unemployment European countries (equations for which are reported in Table 5) and all countries taken together (Table 4).[21] Although these tests point to some significant differences, a comparison of the equations reported in Tables 4 and 5 suggests that this "statistical significance" may reflect the large number of observations rather than important differences in wage formation between the two groups of countries.

Table 6. Tests for differences in wage formation in high-unemployment European countries compared to other countries
(Figures are F-statistics based on the equations reported in tables 4 and 5, *s indicate significance at the 5% level)

Manufacturing		Services		Other	
Total	1.04	Total	1.59*	Mining	0.27
Food	0.57	Trade	1.29	Construction	0.76
Textiles	1.37	Transportation	1.59*	Agriculture	1.04
Paper	0.91	FIRE	1.21	Government	1.61*
Chemicals	1.51*	CS & P	0.63		
Primary metals	1.21				
Mach. & other equip.	0.8				
	1.29				

Notes: The F-tests are for the restriction that the estimated coefficients are the same for high-unemployment European countries (Table 5) and the other countries (Table 4). The critical value at the 1% confidence level is 1.65.

5 Summary

As would be suggested by insider-outsider/hysteresis models of wage formation, annual employment developments can be characterised as a random walk. This is true at the industry, sectoral and aggregate level in all industrialized economies. Another result from the empirical analysis is that industry and sectoral wages are

[21] The F-tests reported in Table 7 are computed as follows:

$F = [(SSE_T - SSE_E) / (n_T - k_T - n_E + k_E)]/[SSE_E/(n_E - k_E)]$ where SSE is the sum of squared residuals, n the number of observations, k the number of independent variables, and subscripts T and E refer to the regressions based on data for all countries and for the high-unemployment European countries, respectively. k_T differs from k_E because of the different number of country-specific intercepts in the two regressions. For $k_T = k_E$ the above reduces to the standard F-test.

importantly affected by aggregate consumer prices as well as by industry and sectoral output prices. Thus at least some economy-wide variables are important to insiders. Aggregate labor-market conditions, as proxied by the unemployment rate, however, appear to have a less pervasive influence on industry wage developments. There is also some evidence that wages in the service sector and service industries are less responsive to aggregate unemployment than are wages in the manufacturing sector and manufacturing industries.

A more important result is that industries and sectors in which wages seem to be determined by a natural rate/Phillips curve model, whereby unemployment in excess of the natural rate exerts continual downward pressure on wage growth, appear to be the exception rather than the rule. In the majority of industries, when analysed for specific countries, wages are not significantly restrained by high or increasing levels of aggregate unemployment, even in the short run. In these industries, real wages tend to be determined primarily by industry-specific employment and productivity developments. When analysed using pooled data for groups of countries, unemployment tends to be more important and affects the level rather than the growth of wages.[22]

The finding that wage formation in many industries is determined primarily by insiders is consistent with institutional features in many economies. The most obvious, of course, is the bargaining strategies of trade unions which is at the heart of the insider-outsider and the real-wage bargaining model. There is also the practice in the Federal Republic of Germany of declaring wage agreements to be generally binding on all workers and enterprises after a certain percentage of workers in a sector have settled; similar mechanisms such as pattern bargaining and wage leadership may be at work in other countries.[23]

One of the novel results reported here is that, at the industry level, hysteresis does not appear to characterise wage formation in the high-unemployment European countries to a greater extent than in North American and Japan. Indeed, there appears to be little difference in wage formation between the high-unemployment European countries compared with the other countries. This suggests that the very different employment experiences since the late 1970s may be more related to other

---

[22] This suggests that industry wages are determined by a combination of insider and outsider influences, which is the result obtained by Nickell and Wadhwani (1988) and Blanchflower *et al.* (1987). The possibility that aggregate employment growth, which may be highly correlated with industry employment growth in some countries, has an important impact on industry wages has not been tested. If this were the case, it would be evidence in favor of hysteresis given that the growth of aggregate employment is approximately equal to the change in the unemployment rate.

[23] Cf. Burda and Sachs (1987). The operation of the unemployment insurance system may also lead to hysteresis if the generosity of unemployment benefits is related to past levels of unemployment, as is the case in Canada (cf. Milbourne *et al.*, 1989) and perhaps other countries.

factors, such as the strength of aggregate demand, than to differences in particular labor-market institutions.

This result seems inconsistent with a number of aggregate studies suggesting that the phenomenon of hysteresis is more important in Europe and Australia than in North America and Japan. A possible explanation of this apparent contradiction is that at the aggregate level, hysteresis-type effects would only become apparent after unemployment had increased and then remained at the new higher plateau, as it has in much of Europe. If, however, unemployment increased and then fell rapidly, as in the United States since the early 1980s, there would not necessarily be any evidence of hysteresis in the aggregate data even if wages in every industry were completely determined by insiders. Another way to make this point is to consider what unemployment in the United States might have been in the absense of expansionary fiscal policies in the 1980s.

These results, of course, must be treated with some caution. They do, however, suggest that cross-country industry data are a fruitful test bed on which to attempt to discriminate between alternative models of wage determination, as suggested by Blanchard (1988). The preliminary analysis reported here could be extended in a number of ways. Further work might expand the equation specification to better account for industry- and country-specific institutions such as incomes policies, the degree of union power, and the length of bargaining cycles rather than relying on the same specification for all industries and countries. Similarly, the role of developments in industry-specific and aggregate profits, capital-labor ratios and total factor productivity might give a better picture of differences in wage determination, and hence in employment, across countries and industries.

References

Blanchard O (1988) "Unemployment: Getting the Questions Right – and Some of the Answers", NBER Working Paper No. 2698 (September)

Blanchard O, Summers L H (1988) "Hysteresis and the European Unemployment Problem", in Cross (1988), pp. 306–64 and in S. Fischer, ed., NBER Macroeconomics Annual, 1986, MIT Press, pp. 65–71

Blanchflower D G, Oswald A J, Garrett M D (1987) "Insider Power in Wage Determination: Part II", mimeo (June)

Burda M, Sachs J (1987) "Institutional Aspects of High Unemployment in the Federal Republic of Germany", NBER Working Paper No. 2241 (May)

Coe D T (1988) "Hysteresis Effects in Aggregate Wage Equations", in Cross, ed. (1988), pp. 284–305

Chan-Lee J H, Coe D T, Prywes M (1987) "Microeconomic Changes and Macroeconomic Wage Disinflation in the 1980s", (OECD Economic Studies (Spring), pp. 121–57

Cross R ed (1988) Unemployment, Hysteresis & the Natural Rate Hypothesis, Oxford: Basil Blackwell

Friedman M (1968) "The Role of Monetary Policy", American Economic Review (March), pp. 1–17

Gordon R J (1988) "Back to the Future: European Unemployment Today Viewed from America in 1939", Brookings Papers on Economic Activity (No. 1), pp. 271–312

Hendry D F (1986) "Econometric Modelling with Cointegrated Variables: An Overview", Oxford Bulletin of Economics and Statistics (No. 3), pp. 201–12

Katz L (1986) "Efficiency Wage Theories: A Partial Evaluation", NBER Working Paper No. 1906 (April)

Kuh E (1967) "A Productivity Theory of Wage Levels – An Alternative to the Phillips Curve", Review of Economic Studies, pp. 333–60

Lindbeck A, Snower D J (1986a) "Wage Setting, Unemployment, and Insider-Outsider Relations", American Economic Review (May), pp. 235–9

Lindbeck A, Snower D J (1986b) "Efficiency Wages versus Insiders and Outsiders", European Economic Review Proceedings, pp. 407–16

Lindbeck A, Snower D J (1988a) "Cooperation, Harassment, and Involuntary Unemployment: An Insider-Outsider Approach", American Economic Review (March), pp. 167–88

Lindbeck A, Snower D J (1988b) "Long-Term Unemployment and Macroeconomic Policy", American Economic Review (May), pp. 38–49

Meyer-zu-Schlochtern F J M (1988) "An International Sectoral Database for Thirteen OECD Countries", OECD ESD Working Papers No. 57 (November)

Milbourne R D, Purvis D D, Scoones W D (1989), "Unemployment Insurance and Unemployment Dynamics", Institute for Economic Research Discussion Paper No. 750, Queen's University (June)

Nickell S (1988) "The Supply Side and Macroeconomic Modeling", in R. Bryant, et al., ed., Empirical Macroeconomics for Interdependent Economies, Brookings Institution

Nickell S, Kong P (1988) "An Investigation into the Power of Insiders in Wage Determination", Oxford Applied Economics Discussion Paper No. 49 (June)

Nickell S, Wadhwani S (1988) "Insider Forces and Wage Determination", Institute of Economics and Statistics, University of Oxford, mimeo (March)

Salop S (1979) "A Model of the Natural Rate of Unemployment", American Economic Review (March), pp. 117–25

Sargan J D (1964) "Wages and Prices in the United Kingdom: A Study in Econometric Methodology", in P.E. Hart, et al., ed., Econometric Analysis for National Economic Planning, London: Butterworths

Sargan J D, Bhargava (1983) "Testing residuals from Least Squares Regression for being Generated by the Gaussian Random Walk", Econometrica (January), pp. 153–74

Snower D J (1988) "European Unemployment: The Insider-Outsider Explanation and its Policy Implications", CEPR Bulletin (June), pp. 3–7

Solow R (1985) "Insiders and Outsiders in Wage Determination", Scandinavian Journal of Economics (No. 2)

Testing for Hysteresis in Unemployment An Unobserved Components Approach[1]

By A. Jaeger[2] and M. Parkinson[3]

Abstract: We suggest a new test for hysteresis in unemployment based on an unobserved components model. Observed unemployment rates are decomposed into a natural rate component and a cyclical component. The impact of lagged cyclical shocks on the current natural component is the measure of hysteresis. To identify the two components of unemployment, we assume that the cyclical compoentn is correlated with capacity utilization. The model is applied to U.S. and German data. We find no evidence of hysteresis in U.S. data. German unemployment rates exhibit substantial hysteresis. A shock of 1.0 percent to the current cyclical component permanently increases future German natural rates by about 0.5 percent. For both countries, natural rate shocks turn out to be an important impulse mechanism to explain movements in observed unemployment rates.

1 Introduction

Over the last 15 years, high and persistent unemployment has surfaced as the major macroeconomic problem in many European economies (in particular in Germany, France, Italy and the United Kingdom) as well as in Australia and Canada. In contrast, the U.S. has experienced large swings in its unemployment rate with an apparent tendency of observed unemployment to move back toward some relatively stable underlying rate. By way of further contrast, Japan and some European economies, notably Austria, Norway, Sweden, and Switzerland, have enjoyed basically stable unemployment rates over the same time period. Explaining this diver-

[1] We would like to thank Ben Bernanke, John Campbell, Whitney Newey, Pierre Perron, Mark Schankerman, and two anonymous referees for helpful comments. All remaining errors are our own. The first author acknowledges financial support by the Erwin Schroedinger Foundation and the second author by the Australian Treasury. The views expressed herein are our own and should not be attributed to the sponsoring bodies.

[2] Albert Jaeger, Institute for Advanced Studies, Stumpergasse 56, A-1060 Vienna, Austria.

[3] Martin Parkinson, Department of Economics, Princeton University, Princeton, NJ 08540, USA, and Australian Treasury, Canberra, ACT 2600, Australia.

sity of experience has put macroeconomic theory to a severe test, and several commentators have already expressed doubt that it has met this challenge adequately (see Blinder 1988).

As a matter of taxonomy, standard theories of unemployment suggest that high observed unemployment can be the result of structural factors that have changed the natural rate of unemployment or of cyclical factors that have temporarily driven unemployment above the natural rate. The relatively low and stable inflation rates of the 1980s are widely interpreted as casting doubt on the possibility that cyclical factors are responsible for high unemployment rates. The pressing question then is: Why have natural rates moved up so sharply in many countries over the last 15 years?

According to one influential view, unemployment increased because the structural determinants of the natural rate changed. Bruno and Sachs (1985) argue that increased „wage gaps“ led to upward pressure on the natural rate in many countries during the 1970s. Layard and Nickell (1986) report that part of the increase in British unemployment can be traced to changes in structural factors including unemployment benefits, employment protection laws, and union militancy. Lindbeck (1985) attributes the increase in natural rates to the debilitating effects of increased government intervention. Coe (1989) investigates Lindbeck's hypothesis for Canada and concludes that the increased generosity of the unemployment insurance system was a major cause for the rise in the natural rate during the 1970s.

The main alternative hypothesis to the structural view is based on the concept of hysteresis in the natural rate. First applied in unambiguous terms to the labor market by Hargreaves Heap (1980), this hypothesis postulates that the natural rate depends on the previous history of unemployment. Three major mechanisms for this historydependence have been suggested – the erosion of human capital due to unemployment, a shortage of physical capital, and so called „insider-outsider“ mechanisms associated with and so called „indider-outsider“ mechanisms associated with wage determination. Blanchard and Summers (1986) and Gordon (1988) find that the hysteresis hypothesis is well supported for several European countries by empirical evidence from wage-price systems. Some supporting evidence is also reported by Franz (1987) for Germany and Gregory (1986) for Australia. Coe (1987) reports mixed results in a study of wage equations for 12 OECD countries.

In this paper we adopt an unobserved components (*UC*) approach to test for hysteresis in unemployment. Unobserved components models have been suggested by Watson and Engle (1983) and Harvey and Todd (1983) as flexible instruments for extracting information from observed variables (e.g. the unemployment rate) regarding the properties of unobservable variables (e.g. the natural unemployment rate). Our application of *UC* models to labor markets is closely related to work by Clark (1989). The basic idea in statistical terms is to disentangle the nonstationary natural rate component and the stationary cyclical component of unemployment by using the information contained in a variable that is correlated with the cyclical component of unemployment. Preferably, the variable used to achieve the decomposition should be stationary to obviate the need to decompose this variable itself into a stationary and nonstationary part. For this reason, we use capacity utilization to identify the decomposition. Other variables such as Gross National Product could be used for the decomposition. The difficulty with GNP, however, is that it is itself nonstationary and has first to be decomposed into a stationary and nonstationary component. Regardless of the variable used to achieve the decomposition of unemployment into its natural and cyclical components, the measure of hysteresis defined in this paper is given by the impact on the current natural rate of lagged cyclical shocks.

We use the *UC* approach to provide information on the importance of hysteresis effects relative to structural factors for explaining persistently high unemployment. The *UC* approach is not a substitute for work that tries to pin down the economic forces behind the movements in the natural rate, but it can provide a clue on where the search for these forces is most likely to be successful.

In the empirical section of the paper we apply the *UC* model to seasonally adjusted quarterly postwar time series on unemployment rates and capacity utilization from the U.S. and Germany, Our results indicate no evidence in favor of hysteresis for U.S. data. For Germany, the results show that shocks to the cyclical component of unemployment have a substantial long term effect on the natural rate. A shock of 1.0 percent to the current cyclical component permanently increases future German natural rates by about 0.5 percent. For both countries, current shocks to the natural rate turn out to be an important impulse mechanism to explain movements in observed unemployment rates.

Section 2 outlines an operational definition of hysteresis in terms of unobserved components of unemployment. Section 3 discusses the estimation of the *UC* model. In section 4, we offer a critical appraisal of alternative approaches to testing hysteresis from the viewpoint of the *UC* approach. Empirical results are presented in section 5, and section 6 concludes.

2 Measuring Hysteresis

Assume the unemployment rate to be the sum of a cyclical („transitory" or „stationary") component, U_t^C, and a natural („permanent" or „nonstationary") component, U_t^N,

$$U_t = U_t^N + U_t^C \ . \tag{1}$$

The cyclical component is assumed to be generated by a stationary process and to follow an autoregressive process of order two with the suitable stationarity conditions imposed on the coefficients ϕ_1 and ϕ_1

$$U_t^C = \phi_1 U_{t-1}^C + \phi_2 U_{t-1}^C + \varepsilon_t^C . \tag{2}$$

The assumption of a second order autoregressive representation for the cyclical component can easily be relaxed, but we find that second order processes typically fit well for the unemployment data used in this paper.

The natural rate component is assumed to evolve as

$$U_t^N = U_{t-1}^N + \varepsilon_t^N + \theta \varepsilon_{t-1}^C , \tag{3}$$

i.e. as a random walk plus the effect of lagged shocks to the cyclical component of unemployment. The coefficient θ measures in percentage points by how much the natural rate increases in all future periods if the economy experiences a 1.0 percent cyclical shock in unemployment. Our measure of hysteresis is analogous to measures of persistence in GNP (see Campbell and Mankiw 1987).

Permanent and cyclical shocks are assumed to be uncorrelated at all leads and lags. The presence of the cyclical shock lagged once in (3) captures the notion that hysteresis occurs if the natural rate is dependent on the history of cyclical shocks. As a special case, the natural rate component may be constant (variance $(\epsilon_t^N) = 0$ and $\theta = 0$). By ruling out a drift term in (3), we a priori exclude the possibility that unemployment follows a deterministic trend. A further restriction imposed by (3) is that permanent shocks, ϵ_t^N, increase the current and all future natural rates by exactly the amount of the current shock. It should be kept in mind that these assumptions will give one possible decomposition of unemployment in its permanent and transitory component. Other researchers might prefer different decompositions on an a priori basis (see Quah 1988).

Measuring hysteresis by the effect of once-lagged cyclical shocks on the current natural rate may not capture physical and human capital channels causing hysteresis adequately if there are long time lags involved before human or physical capital decays. In principle, the model could be generalized by including higher lags of the cyclical shock in (3) and by imposing a distributed lag structure on the generalized model (e.g. a Koyck lag structure). The model as adopted in this paper should be able to capture hysteresis effects working through insider-outsider mechanisms in wage bargaining (see Lindbeck and Snower 1986). The insider-outsider hypothesis asserts in its most simplified form that wages are set by bargaining between firms and their employees (the insiders) without regard for the unemployed (the outsiders). The employed wish to ensure to remain employed but have no interest in ensuring the employment of the outsiders. The major implication of the insider-outsider hypothesis is that in response to an adverse shock which reduces employment some of the previous insiders become outsiders and the new, smaller, group of insiders sets the wage to ensure the new lower level of employment. Hence any given cyclical shock to unemployment will at least be partially permanent, raising next period's natural rate.

3 Estimation of the Unobserved Components Model

The discussion of identification of *UC* models in Watson (1986) shows that the system (1) to (3) is not identified because the cyclical and the permanent component are neither perfectly correlated nor uncorrelated. Additional identifying information bearing either on the cyclical or the permenent component of unemployment has to be brought into the model. We use capacity utilization (CU_t) to pick up the movements in the cyclical component of unemployment. Capacity utilization is assumed to be stationary, an assumption that will be tested below, and to be correlated with the cyclical component in unemployment.

To estimate the model, we write it in state space form. The transition equations are set up as

$$\begin{bmatrix} U_t^N \\ U_t^C \\ U_{t-1}^C \\ F_t \end{bmatrix} = \begin{bmatrix} 1 & 0 & 0 & 1 \\ 0 & \phi_1 & \phi_2 & 0 \\ 0 & 1 & 0 & 0 \\ 0 & 0 & 0 & 0 \end{bmatrix} \begin{bmatrix} U_{t-1}^N \\ U_{t-1}^C \\ U_{t-2}^C \\ F_{t-1} \end{bmatrix} + \begin{bmatrix} \varepsilon_t^N \\ \varepsilon_t^C \\ 0 \\ \theta\varepsilon_t^C \end{bmatrix} \tag{4}$$

Writing out the transition equations (4) in equation form and substitution shows that (4) is equivalent to equations (2) and (3). The measurement equations are given by

$$\begin{bmatrix} U_t \\ CU_t \end{bmatrix} = \begin{bmatrix} 1 & 1 & 0 & 0 \\ 0 & a_0 & a_1 & 0 \end{bmatrix} \begin{bmatrix} U_t^N \\ U_t^C \\ U_{t-1}^C \\ F_t \end{bmatrix} + \begin{bmatrix} 0 \\ v_t \end{bmatrix} \tag{5}$$

The shock v_t denotes a measurement error in the equation linking capacity utilization and cyclical unemployment. The variance-covariance matrix (Σ) of the three shocks is given by

$$\Sigma = \begin{bmatrix} \sigma_N^2 & 0 & 0 \\ 0 & \sigma_C^2 & 0 \\ 0 & 0 & \sigma_v^2 \end{bmatrix} \tag{6}$$

and the cyclical component but found this type of correlation to be insignificant in our empirical work with U.S. and German data. All shocks are assumed to be uncorrelated over time and normally distributed.

The parameters to be estimated are ϕ_1, ϕ_2, θ, a_0, a_1, σ_N^2, σ_C^2, and σ_V^2. We use the Kalman filter to calculate the likelihood for observing a sample of observations on unemployment and capacity utilization given a fixed parameter vector. Harvey (1981, chapter 4) is a straightforward guide for setting up the prediction and updating equations of the Kalman filter. The likelihood is maximized by the method of scoring with modified step size suggested in Berndt et. al. (1974). The program used for estimation is written in GAUSS.

4 Alternative Approaches for Testing Hysteresis

The *UC* approach provides a useful perspective for a critical appraisal of other approaches for testing hysteresis. The *UC* approach suggests that all tests of hysteresis must at least implicitly disentangle the cyclical and natural component in unemployment by using information in variables that move either with the natural or the cyclical component. From this point of view it follows immediately that the univariate properties of the observed unemployment series, e.g. the persistence of unemployment, can provide no information on the existence of hysteresis effects. High persistence of unemployment can be due either to natural rate shocks or hysteresis effects or both.

Most authors have taken the following stylized approach for testing hysteresis (see the discussion of Franz 1987 by Wyplosz 1987). A Phillips curve is postulated

$$\pi_t = \pi_t^e + \beta(U_t^N - U_t)\,, \tag{7}$$

where π_t and π_t^e are the actual and expected rates of inflation. Other variables may be included without affecting the argument. The natural rate is assumed to be determined by

$$U_t^N = cU_{t-1} + bZ_t\,. \tag{8}$$

The vector Z_t contains variables explaining shifts in the natural rate due to „structural factors“. The vector of structural factors, Z, may include changes in the composition of the labour force by demographic and skill category (what is commonly referred to as „mismatch“) and causes of distortions in the labour market such as unemployment replacement ratios, minimum wages, labour taxes, employment security legislation, and social obstacles to labour mobility. Inserting

(8) into (7) gives

$$\pi_t = \pi_t^e - \beta U_t + \beta c U_{t-1} + \beta b Z_t \,. \tag{9}$$

The hypothesis $c = 1$ is taken to represent the case of a „hysteresis economy". To discuss the properties of this test it is useful to rewrite (9) with the unemployment rate as the dependent variable

$$U_t = cU_{t-1} + bZ_t + (1/\beta)(\pi_t - \pi_t^e) \tag{10}$$

We note the following properties of this alternative test for hysteresis:

First, the hysteresis hypothesis is a point hypothesis. It corresponds to the extreme hypothesis $\theta = 1$ in the *UC* approach. Past shocks to cyclical unemployment are assumed to be fully reflected in the natural rate.

Second, from equation (10) we see that the test $c = 1$ is basically a unit root test. The test does not supply a measure of the economic significance of hysteresis. From the literature on unit roots in GNP we know that the finding of a unit root gives no indication of the economic significance of permanent shocks to GNP (see Campbell and Mankiw 1987).

Third, the statistical distributions of the estimates from the Phillips curve approach are presumably nonstandard. If we assume the unemployment rate to have a unit root and $b = 0$, the test is biased against finding hysteresis since under the null of $c = 1$ the critical values for the resulting test statistic must be taken from Fuller (1976) and not, as is usual practice, from the standard Student-*t* distribution. Furthermore, if the natural rate is in fact shifted by a vector of presumably nonstationary variables Z_t, i.e. b is different from zero, the relevant distributions of the test statistics of the coefficients c and b might also be nonstandard.

Fourth, the Phillips curve approach works by using „information variables", Z_t, correlated with the natural rate. Failue to specify Z_t correctly, or not at all as in Blanchard and Summers (1986), will lead to finding hysteresis by default if unemployment has a unit root. If Z_t is correctly specified, however, the Phillips curve approach could in principle provide the relevant information for economic policy on what actually moved the natural rate.

5 Empirical Results

The empirical analysis uses seasonally adjusted, quarterly data for the U.S. and Germany. The sample period for the U.S. data is 1954.1 to 1989.1. Data for the unemployment rate are from various issues of the Bureau of Labor Statistics Bulletin. Data on capacity utilization are taken from various issues of the Fedcral Reserve

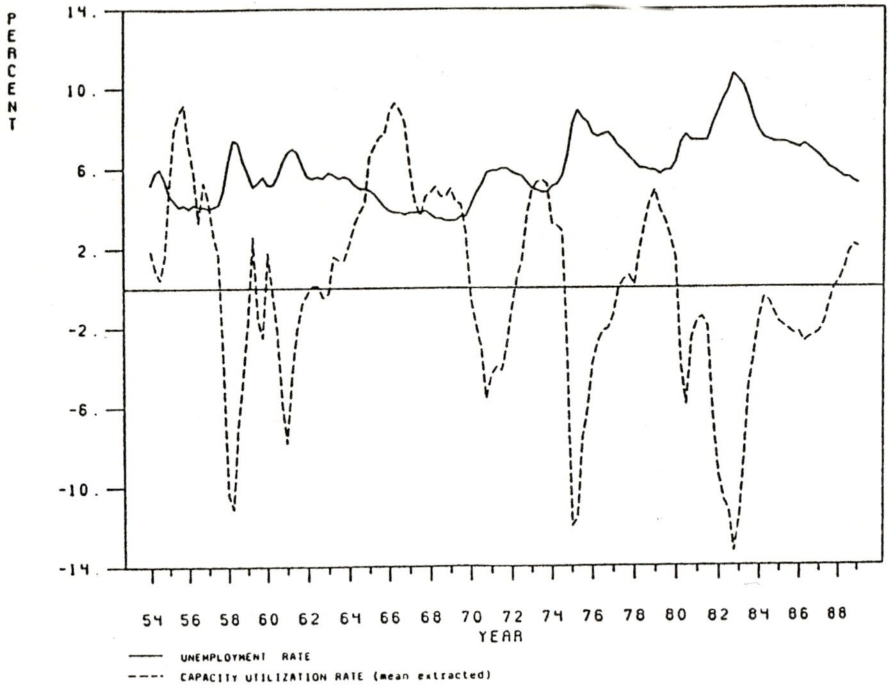

Fig. 1a. U.S. Unemployment and capacity utilization. 1954.1–1989.1

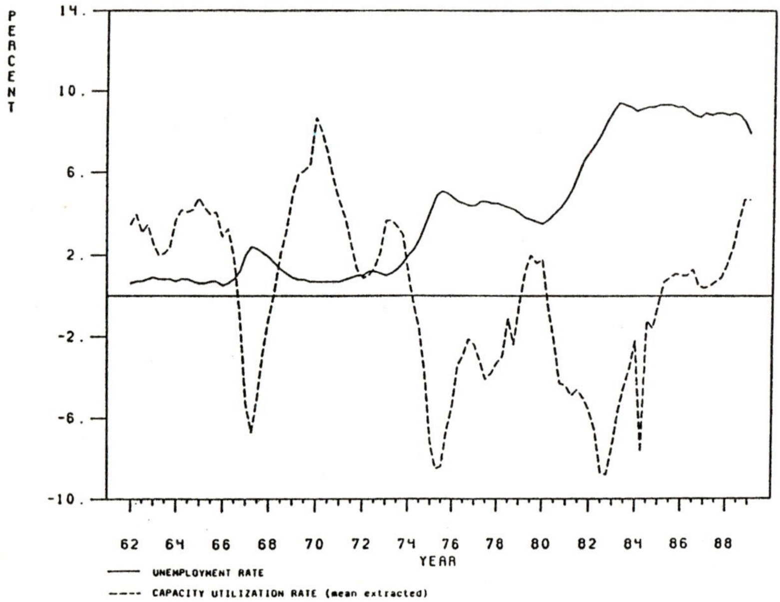

Fig. 1b. German unemployment and capazity utilization. 1962.1–1989.1

Table 1. Augmented Dickey-Fuller (ADF) tests for unit roots[a]

A.) U.S. Data: 1954.1-1989.1

Unemployment Rate

$$\Delta U_t = \underset{(.11)}{.24} - \underset{(.02)}{.04}U_{t-1} + \underset{(.08)}{.78}\Delta U_{t-1} - \underset{(.09)}{.22}\Delta U_{t-2}$$

$R^2 = .46$ ADF = -2.43

Capacity Utilization

$$\Delta CU_t = \underset{(2.89)}{9.22} - \underset{(.04)}{.11}CU_{t-1} + \underset{(.08)}{.59}\Delta CU_{t-1} - \underset{(.10)}{.27}\Delta CU_{t-2} + \underset{(.09)}{.26}\Delta CU_{t-3} - \underset{(.09)}{.17}\Delta CU_{t-4}$$

$R^2 = .34$ ADF = -3.21

B. German Data: 1962.1-1989.1

Unemployment Rate

$$\Delta U_t = \underset{(.03)}{.04} - \underset{(.005)}{.008}U_{t-1} + \underset{(.06)}{.82}\Delta U_{t-1}$$

$R^2 = .64$ ADF = -1.02

Capacity Utilization

$$\Delta CU_t = \underset{(2.86)}{8.75} - \underset{(.03)}{.11}CU_{t-1} + \underset{(.09)}{.19}\Delta CU_{t-1} + \underset{(.09)}{.32}\Delta CU_{t-2}$$

$R^2 = .18$ ADF = -3.07

[a] Standard errors in parentheses below coefficient estimates. Critical values for argumented Dickey-Fuller test statistic (ADF) from Fuller (1976, p. 373) are –3.51 (1%), –2.89 (5%), and –2.58 (10%).

Bulletin. Figure la plots the U.S. unemployment rate and the mean adjusted capacity utilization rate. The unemployment and capacity utilization series for Germany run from 1962.1 to 1989.1. These data are taken from OECD Main Economic Indicators. Because the German capacity utilization series is seasonally unadjusted we have adjusted the series by Census $X-11$. The German series are plotted in figure 1b. The capacity utilization series refer to the manufacturing sector, and figures 1a and 1b suggest a close inverse relationship between these series and the unemployment rates for both countries.

Table 2. Estimates for unobserved components models

U.S.A. 1954.1 - 1989.1

Log Likelihood 76.32

Parameters	ϕ_1	1.63	(.05)
	ϕ_2	-.72	(.06)
	θ	.11	(.09)
	a_0	-.79	(.06)
	a_1	.36	(.05)
	σ_N =	.18	
	σ_C =	.23	
	σ_V =	.004	

Likelihood Ratio Test (Null: $\theta = 0$) 2.34[b]

Germany 1962.1 - 1989.1

Log Likelihood 82.97

Parameters	ϕ_1	1.78	(.08)
	ϕ_2	-.83	(.07)
	θ	.50	(.30)
	a_0	-1.38	(.26)
	a_1	.93	(.28)
	σ_P =	.18	
	σ_C =	.09	
	σ_V =	.03	

Likelihood Ratio Test (Null $\theta = 0$) 4.29[b]

[a] Capacity utilization has been scaled by a factor of 10. Asymptotic standard errors in parentheses.
[b] Distributed as Chi-Square with 1 degree of freedom under the null. Critical values are 6.63 (1%), 3.84 (5%), and 2.71 (10%).

As a first step, we test two important assumptions concerning the stationarity properties of the variables in the *UC* model. Unemployment should have a unit root in levels while capacity utilization should be stationary in levels. We test for unit roots using augmented Dickey-Fuller tests. Starting with regressions including 6 lagged autoregressive terms, lags insignificant at the 5 percent level were eliminated in a stepwise regression procedure starting with the highest lag. Table 1 reports the results with only the significant lags included. The null of a unit root can not be rejected for the unemployment rates even at the 10 percent significance level. Capacity utilization measures are judged stationary at the conventional 5 percent significance level.

We excluded a time trend from the Dickey-Fuller regressions on the assumption that neither unemployment nor capacity utilization is deterministically growing or falling over time. This point is important since other researchers appear to assume the unemployment rate to have a deterministic trend (see e.g. Blanchard and Quah 1988 and Clark 1989). We find the assumption of a deterministic upward or downward trend in unemployment unattractive on an a priori basis.

Table 2 reports estimates of the parameters and test statistics for the *UC* model. We first discuss the U.S. results.

The point estimate of the hysteresis coefficient θ for the U.S. is 0.11 A likelihood ratio test of the hypothesis that $\theta = 0.0$ cannot reject the null even at the 10 percent level. This finding suggests that hysteresis effects in the U.S. unemployment rate are neither economically important nor statistically significant. These results are consistent with conventional wisdom in the sense that they suggest a U.S. natural unemployment rate that is shifted over time by structural facgtors with large but independent movements of the actual unemployment rate around the natural rate. In figure 2a, we plot the natural rate component of U.S. unemployment derived from smoothed Kalman filter estimates along with the actual unemployment rate. As an aside, we note from figure 2a that by the time the Kennedy-Johnson tax cuts were implemented as a countercyclical measure in February 1964, the actual rate of unemployment was already below the natural rate. By contrast, the Reagan Economic Recovery Tax Act of 1981 introduced tax cuts which took effect in 1982, a time when the actual unemployment rate exceeded the natural rate by more than two percentage points.

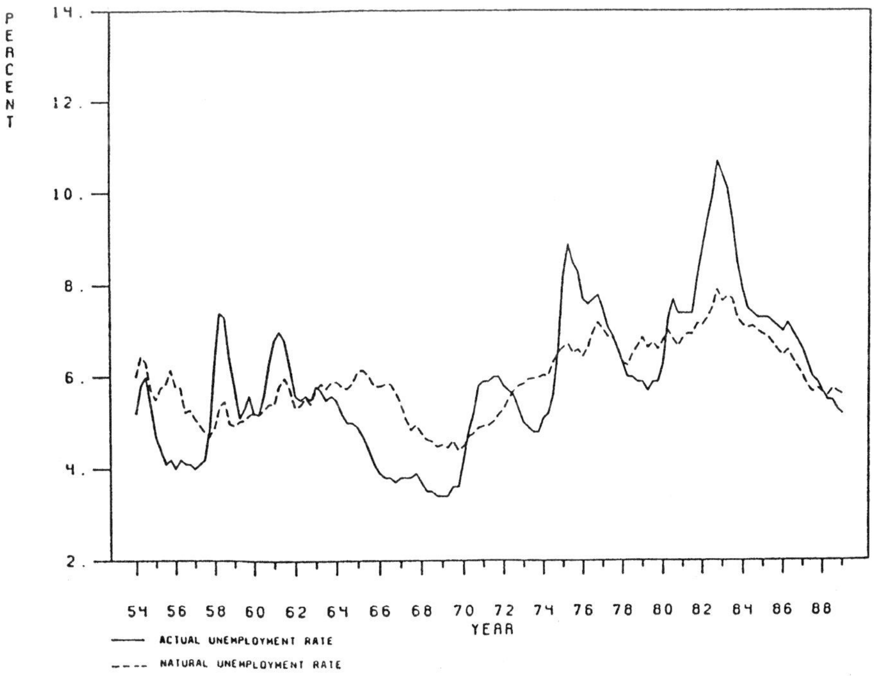

Fig. 2a. U.S. Actual and natural unemployment rate. 1954.1–1989.1

The results for Germany suggest a different interpretation. The hysteresis coefficient θ is estimated to be about 0.50, implying that a positive 1 percent shock in cyclical unemployment will increase future natural rates by about 0.50 percent. A likelihood ratio test of $\theta = 0.0$ rejects the null at the 5 percent significance level but not at a 1 percent level. We conclude from these results that the evidence in a formal statistical sense is not overwhelming but accepting the point estimate of θ would indicate substantial hysteresis in the German unemployment rate. It is important to note, however, that hysteresis is only a partial explanation for the increase in the German natural rate given the substantial variance of the shocks to the natural rate. Figure 2b plots the natural and actual unemployment rate for Germany.

In both countries, a 1 percent change in cyclical unemployment is associated with a steady state change in capacity utilization of some 4 percent. Judging from the standard deviation of measurement error in the equation linking capacity utilization and cyclical unemployment (σ_v), movements in the U.S. cyclical component appear to be much more closely related to capacity utilization than in the German case.

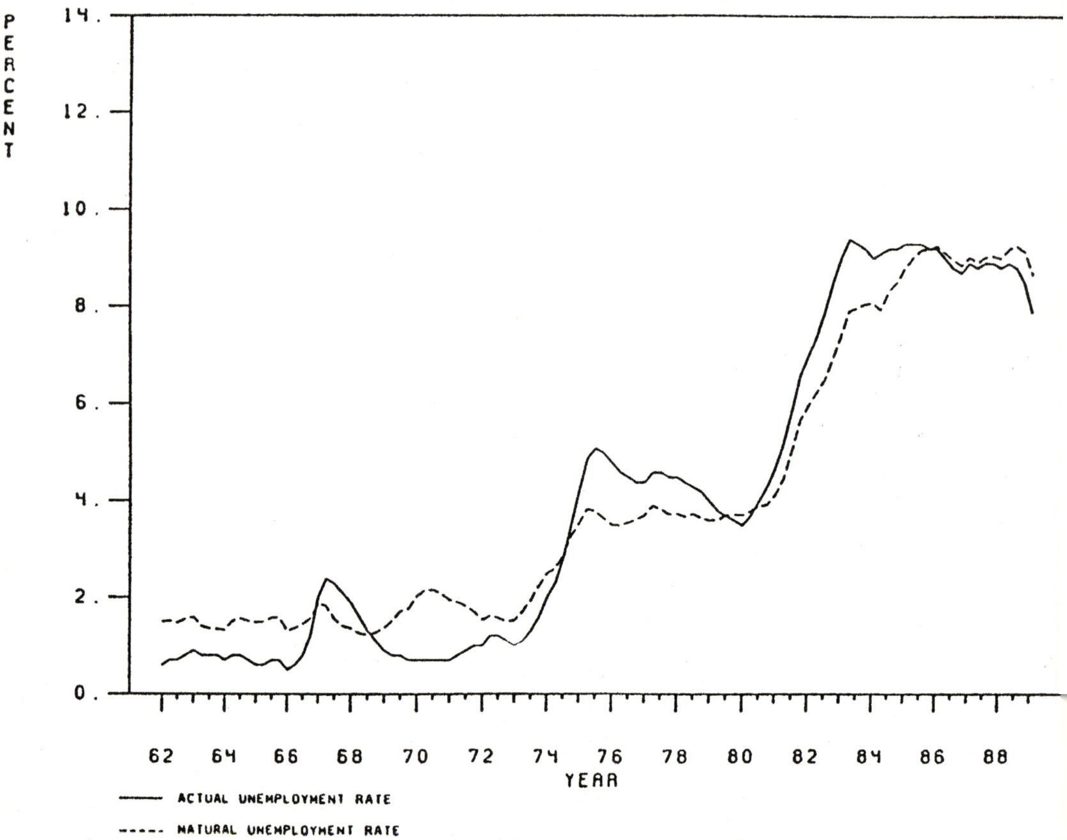

Fig. 2b. German actual and natural unemployment rate. 1962.1–1989.1

6 Conclusion

We suggested in this paper a new test for hysteresis in unemployment. The observed unemployment rate is decomposed into a natural rate component and a cyclical component. The impact of lagged cyclical shocks on the current natural component supplies a measure of hysteresis. The empirical results for U.S. and German data provide no evidence for hysteresis in the U.S. unemployment rate but an economically significant hysteresis effect for the German unemployment rate. A shock of 1.0 percent to the current cyclical component permanently increases future German natural rates by about 0.5 percent. For both countries, current shocks to the natural rate turn out to be an important impulse mechanism to explain movements in observed unemployment rates.

References

Berndt E K, Hall R E, Hall B H, Hausman J (1974) Estimation and inference in nonlinear structural models. Annals of Economic and Social Measurement 3:653–66

Blanchard O J, Quah D (1988) The dynamic effects of aggregate demand and supply disturbances. NBER Working Paper No. 2737

Blanchard O J, Summers L H (1986) Hysteresis and the European unemployment problem. NBER Macroeconomics Annual 1986, MIT Press

Blinder A S (1988) The challenge of high unemployment. American Economic Review 78: 1–15

Bruno M, Sachs JD (1985) Economics of Worldwise Stagflation. Harvard University Press

Campbell J Y, Mankiw NG (1987) Are output fluctuations transitory? Quarterly Journal of Economics 102: 857–880

Clark P K (1989) Trend reversion in real output and unemployment. Journal of Econometrics, 40:15–32

Coe D T (1988) Hysteresis Effects in Aggregate Wage Equations. In: R Cross (ed.) Unemployment, Hysteresis and the Natural Rate Hypothesis, Basil Blackwell

Coe D T (1989) Structural determinants of the natural rate of unemployment in Canada. IMF Working Paper.

Franz W (1987) Hysteresis, persistence, and the NAIRU: An empirical analysis for the Republic of Germany In: R Layard, L Calmfors (eds.) The Fight Against Unemployment, Centre for European Policy Studies, MIT Press

Fuller W A (1976) Introduction to Statistical Time Series. John Wiley & Sons

Gordon R J (1988) Back to the future: European unemployment today viewed from America in 1939. Brooking Papers on Economic Activity 19:1271–312

Gregory R G (1986) Wage policy and unemployment in Australia. Economica (Supplement): 53–74

Hargreaves Heap S P (1980) Choosing the wrong natural rate, accelerating inflation or decelerating unemployment and growth? Economic Journal 90: 611–20

Harvey A C (1981) Time Series Models. Philip Allan

Harvey A C, Todd P H J (1983) Forecasting economic time series with structural and Box-Jenkins models: A case study. Journal of Business and Economic Statistics, 1:299–315

Layard R, Nickell S J (1986) Unemployment in Britain. Economica 53 (Supplement): 121–170

Lindbeck A (1985) What is wrong with the West European economies? World Economy 8: 153–70

Lindbeck A, Snower D J (1986) Wage setting, unemployment and insider-outsider relations. American Economic Review 76/2:235–39

Quah D (1988) The relative importance of permanent and transitory components: identification and some theoretical bounds. mimeo, MIT.

Watson M W (1986) Univariate detrending methods with stochastic trends. Journal of Monetary Economics 18:49–76

Watson M W, Engle R E (1983) Alternative algorithms for the estimation of dynamic factor, MIMIC, and varying coefficient regression models. Journal of Econometrics, 23:385–400

Wyplosz C (1987) Comments. In: R Layard, L Calmfors (eds.) The Fight Against Unemployment, Centre for European Policy Studies, MIT Press

Unemployment and Deterioration of Human Capital

A Labour Market Model with Hysteresis Implications

By J. Möller[1]

Abstract: The paper deals with the deterioration of human capital during spells of unemployment. In our model the probability of leaving the unemployment pool decreases with the duration of unemployment. It can be shown that with a linear deterioration function and a simple distribution function for the reservation productivity of firms, unemployment duration is suitably described by a distribution of the Gompertz-Makeham type. In a numerical simulation it could be demonstrated that deterioration of human capital during unemployment affects the relation between vacancies and unemployment in a specific way: in the case of labour market slackness the steady-state Beveridge curve bends away markedly from the standard u-v-curve in an outward direction while in a situation of almost full employment the effects are negligible. For higher deterioration parameters the Beveridge curve may even be upward sloping in a situation of excess supply on the labour market, implying the existence of multiple equilibria. Empirical estimation of the distribution function with German labour market data 1984–1987 reveals that the multiple equilibrium case is likely to be relevant in reality.

1 Introduction

In their famous article about 'Hysteresis and the European Unemployment Problem', Blanchard and Summers list three different approaches which can be adduced to explain why shocks that cause unemployment might have long-term effects: shortage of physical capital, the insider-outsider approach and human capital theories. The first two theories have been elaborated by several authors [see, for example, Blanchard, Summers (1986), Lindbeck, Snower (1986b, 1987a,b), Gottfries, Horn (1987) for the insider-outsider models, Burda (1988) for the capital shortage approach]. The human capital approach, however, has attracted much less theoretical interest, despite the contributions of Phelps (1972) and Hargraves Heap (1980), pointing out that unemployment may have important effects on the skills

[1] Joachim Möller, Fakultät für Wirtschaftswissenschaften, Universität Konstanz, Postfach 5560, D-7750 Konstanz.
For valuable comments and suggestions I am grateful to W.Franz, A.Hamerle and an anonymous referee. Responsibility for remaining errors remains with the author.

and motivation of the unemployed which affect the matching process and labour supply in general.

One argument against the relevance of the insider-outsider story is the observation that hysteresis seems to be a phenomenon of 'bad times' rather than of 'good times', i.e. persistent effects of adverse shocks are more likely to occur in an environement where a tendency to overall excess supply on the labour market prevails rather than in an economy which is geared to full employment. For example, why should insiders have acted completly different in the (severe, but short-lived) German recession of 1966/67 than in 1974/75 or in 1980/81 where much more persistent effects on unemployment were observed? An approach which concentrates on wage-setting behaviour in response to shocks has little to say with respect to this important discrepancy, so the insider-outsider aspect is not the complete story. Burda (1988) stresses another point which also is important for the understanding of the specific German situation: between 1980 and 1983 real wage income has been *declining* while unemployment has been rising. He presents a theoretical model which reconciles this empirical observation with an optimising model of wage-setting behavior in the presence of capital shortage. In our view, human capital aspects are equally important.

It is a well-established empirical fact that the probability of leaving the unemployment pool falls essentially with longer duration of unemployment. Basically there are two – in our view complementary – lines of argument to rationalise this phenomenon. The first approach [see for example Budd, Levine, Smith (1987, 1988) and Tötsch (1988)] stresses the role of heterogeneity between workers: During periods of high unemployment a sorting mechanism is at work which leaves behind the less qualified so that groups with unfavourable characteristics appear to be over-represented in the unemployment pool. The second approach assumes a depreciation process for human capital during spells of unemployment, because the 'workers who are unemployed lose the opportunity to maintain and update their skills by working' [Blanchard, Summers (1986, p. 28)]. From the standpoint of hysteresis theory both approaches lead to consequences which are more or less equivalent: in case of the sorting effect, persistent slackness of labour markets causes social costs in the form of generating problem groups on the labour market and in case of the depreciation effect social costs arise from the loss of human capital. Also, since from the two different approaches very similar effects on the matching process can be expected, no attempt is made in the present paper to disentangle sorting and duration effects empirically. But in the theoretical model an explicit deterioration process of human capital is assumed.

The paper is organised as follows: In the next section a probabilistic model of the matching process is developed. We then derive the steady-state Beveridge curve and analyse the effects of an increasing 'depreciation rate of human capital' by means of a numerical simulation. The final section provides some estimation results for German labour market data.

2 A Probabilistic Model of the Matching Process

In order to keep the model tractable, several simplifications are made. First of all it is assumed that the working force of a representative labour market is homogeneous in the status of employment but inhomogeneous in the status of unemployment since human capital deteriorates during unemployment. The deterioration only concerns those components of human capital which are perishable (for example those aquired by experience rating) but do not affect basic skills.

Since we are primarily interested in analysing a situation of excess supply on the labour market the failure of an unemployed person to get a job is considered in more detail than the failure of a vacancy to be filled. Let us simply assume that vacancies which are unfilled after one period are independently re-announced in the next. The total number of vacancies per period is taken as exogenous to our model.

Firms differ in the extent to which the perishable components of human capital play a role for the productivity of their employees. Thus, each vacancy is associated with a specific qualification standard, expressed as a maximum tolerable duration of unemployment of the candidate.[2] A contact between an employer and an applicant is successful (leads to an employment contract) if the applicant meets this standard.

Applicants for a job are randomly drawn from the unemployment register. It is possible that an unemployed person gets more than one chance per period, i.e. a probabilistic model with repetition is applied. For the search process of the worker a very simple stopping rule is chosen, which might be regarded as realistic in slack labour markets: the first possibility of getting a job is accepted. If a firm contacts a person who was in the unemployment register at the beginning of the time period but in the meantime has been successful, the corresponding vacancy remains unfilled.

The probability that a specific unemployed person is contacted for a specific vacancy is $1/U$, where U is the total number of the unemployed. Thus, the probability that an unemployed person has no contact if there are V vacancies in the period under consideration is $(1-1/U)^V$. Since $1/U$ is a small number, this probability can be rewritten by using the approximation $\ln(1-1/U) \approx -1/U$ as

$$\left(1-\frac{1}{U}\right)^V \approx e^{-k} \qquad (1)$$

where k denotes the ratio between vacancies and unemployment which characterises the labour market situation. If the unemployed – as has been assumed in traditional

[2] This assumption could also be justified by the argument that employers take the length of the unemployment period as a negative screening device, because they suppose that a selection mechanism is at work which leaves behind the less qualified.

matching models – are homogeneous, the probability λ for a specific person of leaving the unemployment register depends on k only

$$\lambda = 1 - e^{k}, \tag{2}$$

with $\partial\lambda/\partial k = e^{-k} > 0$ and $\partial^2\lambda/\partial k^2 = -e^{-k} < 0$.

It is assumed that human capital deteriorates during unemployment according to a function $h(q)$ with $\partial h(q)/\partial q < 0$ where q is the duration of unemployment. More specifically, the following linear function for the development of human capital during unemployment is chosen for sake of simplicity:

$$h(q) = \max\,[h_0(1 - rq), \bar{h}], \tag{3}$$

where r is a depreciation parameter, h_0 is the human capital of the employed workers and $\bar{h} < h_0$ is the non-perishable part of human capital which remains after a critical duration of unemployment $\bar{q}$ has been exceeded. Let us define unemployment up to duration $\bar{q}$ as 'short-term unemployment' and unemployment with duration $q > \bar{q}$ as 'long-term unemployment'. In the following, we first concentrate on short-term unemployment.

Short-Term Unemployment

Let $F[h(q)]$ be the distribution function of the productivity requirement of the vacancies with $F[h(0)] = 1$. If unemployment duration affects human capital then the event that an unemployed person is drawn from the unemployment register by a searching firm is no longer a guarantee that he or she gets the job. The probability that the employer refuses a contract because of inferior qualification of the applicant depends positively on the duration of unemployment and is

$$1 - F[h(q)]. \tag{4}$$

The probability for an unemployed person to be drawn x times from the unemployment pool is given by the Binomial distribution

$$p(x;\,k) = \binom{V}{x}\left(\frac{1}{U}\right)^{x}\left(1-\frac{1}{U}\right)^{V-x} \tag{5}$$

with mean $V/U = k$. Since k is a relatively small number and there are V 'drawings' (where V is a large number), the Binomial distribution is suitably approximated by the Poisson-distribution:

$$p(x;\, k) \approx \frac{k^x}{x!} e^{-k} \tag{6}$$

For an unemployed person with x contacts the probability of being not accepted by the job-offering firms is $p(x;\, k)\, [1 - F(\cdot)]^x$. Hence the hazard rate, i.e. the probability that an unemployed person with duration q leaves the unemployment register is

$$\lambda(q) = 1 - \sum_{x=0}^{V} p(x;\, k)\, \{1 - F[h(q)]\}^x, \tag{7}$$

where $p(x;\, k)$ is the probability function of the Poisson distribution for a given vacancy-unemployment ratio k. As can be verified easily, the hazard rate λ is a non-increasing function in q and r. Since $F(q) = 1$ for all q if there is no depreciation of human capital ($r = 0$), eq. (7) covers eq. (2) as a special case. The second term on the right side of eq. (7) is a Maclaurin series, so the following approximation can be used for the hazard rate

$$\lambda(q) \approx 1 - e^{-k}\, e^{k(1-F[h(q)])} = 1 - e^{-kF[h(q)]}. \tag{8}$$

Now the unemployment distribution over time for a given labour market situation is analysed. In each period U_0 persons newly enter unemployment, while some of the unemployed leave the register with probability $\lambda = \lambda(q;\, k, r)$. The size of a cohort of unemployed persons with duration q is

$$U(q) = U_0\, e^{-\int_0^q \lambda(\tilde{q})\, \mathrm{d}\tilde{q}}. \tag{9}$$

Since the probability of leaving unemployment is non-negative and declining with q for $r > 0$, eq. (9) is a non-increasing function in q and convex to the origin. Of course, the probability of leaving the unemployment pool is higher in the absence of deterioration of human capital during unemployment for all $q > 0$.

Let the reservation productivity of the firms (in terms of human capital) be identically distributed within the interval $[0, h_0]$. If human capital deteriorates according to a linear function, the distribution function of qualification requirements of the labour-seeking firms can be expressed as

$$F[h(q)] = \max[h(q) / h_0, 0] = \max[1 - rq, 0]. \tag{10}$$

Without loss of generality, it is assumed in the following that the human capital of a person just becoming unemployed (h_0) equals unity. *Figure 1* illustrates the depreciation of human capital depending on unemployment duration q and the corresponding distribution function of productivity reservation. An unemployed person with duration q_1 gets a contract with probability $F[h(q_1)]$, if chosen from the unemployment pool.

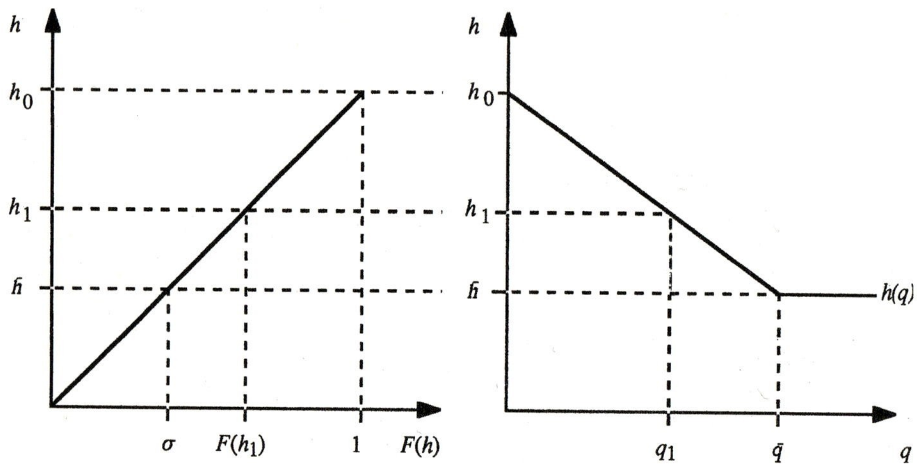

Fig. 1.
a) Distribution of the reservation productivity of firms (in terms of human capital)
b) Deterioration of human capital depending on the duration of unemployment.

These specifications lead to a distribution function for unemployment duration of the Gompertz-Makeham type.[3] This distribution function implies a hazard function of the general form $\lambda(q) = \alpha + \beta \exp(\gamma q)$. In our specific case the parameters are $\alpha = 1$, $\beta = -\exp(-k)$ and $\gamma = kr$. Given a positive depreciation parameter r, the cumulative hazard function can be written as follows:

$$\begin{aligned} L(q) &= \int_0^q \lambda(\tilde{q})\, d\tilde{q} \\ &= q - e^{-k} \int_0^q e^{kr\tilde{q}}\, d\tilde{q} \\ &= q - \frac{1}{kr} e^{-k} (e^{krq} - 1), \end{aligned} \tag{11}$$

[3] See, for example, Blossfeld et al. (1989).

and the 'survivor function' is

$$S(q) = \exp[-L(q)] = \exp[-q - \frac{1}{kr}e^{-k}(1 - e^{krq})]. \tag{12}$$

Total short-term unemployment is determined by the integral over the survivor function

$$U^{st} = U_0 \int_0^{\bar{q}} S(q)\, \mathrm{d}q. \tag{13}$$

Since $L(q)$ is an exponential function in q, the integral in eq. (13) can not be solved analytically.

Long-Term Unemployment

After each period a fraction of the unemployed exceeds duration $\bar{q}$ and enters long-term unemployment. The size of this group is given by

$$U(\bar{q}) = U_0\, e^{-L(\bar{q})}. \tag{14}$$

Let the chance that a long-term unemployed will be accepted if drawn from the unemployment register be

$$\sigma \equiv F[h(\bar{q})] = \frac{\bar{h}}{h_0}. \tag{15}$$

The critical duration of unemployment which separates short-term from long-term unemployment can then be expressed as $\bar{q} = (1 - \sigma)/r$. Substituting this relation in eq. (12) yields

$$L(\bar{q}) = \bar{q}\left[1 - \frac{1}{(1-\sigma)k}(e^{-\sigma k} - e^{-k})\right]. \tag{16}$$

The probability of leaving long-term unemployment by getting a job, is a function of k and σ only:

$$\bar{\lambda} = 1 - e^{-k\sigma}. \tag{17}$$

Solving the expression for total long–term unemployment by partial integration leads to

$$U^{lt} = U(\bar{q}) \int_{\bar{q}}^{\infty} e^{-(1-e^{k\sigma})(\tilde{q}-\bar{q})} \mathrm{d}\tilde{q}$$

$$= \frac{U(\bar{q})}{1-e^{-k\sigma}}, \tag{18}$$

where it has to be assumed that $\sigma > 0$.

Mean Duration of Unemployment and the Loss of Human Capital

If human capital deteriorates during periods of unemployment, hysteresis effects occur in response to shocks in the demand for labour because the term structure of unemployment is affected. The longer the mean duration of unemployment, the higher the loss in human capital and the less likely is that an unemployed person which is randomly drawn from the unemployment pool meets the reservation productivity of a labour-seeking firm.

If $g(q)$ is the density function for the distribution of unemployment, then the mean duration of unemployment can be expressed as

$$m_q = \int_0^{\infty} g(q)\, q \,\mathrm{d}q. \tag{19}$$

For the special case $r = 0$ the integral is easily solved:

$$m_q = \frac{1}{1-e^{-k}}. \tag{20}$$

Hence if human capital does not deteriorate during unemployment, mean duration of unemployment simply is a decreasing convex function in the vacancy-unemployment ratio k.

In the case $r > 0$, mean duration of unemployment is the weighted average duration of the short-term and long-term unemployed

$$m_q = G(\bar{q})\, m_q^{st} + [1 - G(\bar{q})]\, m_q^{lt}, \tag{21}$$

where $G(\cdot) = \int g(q)\, \mathrm{d}q$ is the distribution function of unemployment, i.e. $G(\bar{q})$ and $1 - G(\bar{q})$ are the shares of short-term resp. long-term unemployment in total unemployment. The mean duration of the long-term unemployed m_q^{lt} is $\bar{q} + 1/(1 - e^{-k\sigma})$ and the mean duration of unemployment of the short-term unemployed m_q^{st} is

$\bar{q} - \int_0^{\bar{q}} G^{st}(q)\, \mathrm{d}q$, where G^{st} is the distribution function of short-term unemployment. Furthermore, let us define $z \equiv \int_0^{\bar{q}} G(q)\, \mathrm{d}q$. This expression is an indicator for the term structure of unemployment up to duration $\bar{q}$: the higher z, the less favourable is the term structure, i.e.\ the more the short-term unemployed are concentrated in groups with (relatively) high duration. Using these definitions and eq. (21) gives the formula

$$m_q = \bar{q} - z + [1 - G(\bar{q}] / \ddot{\lambda}\ , \tag{22}$$

since $G^{st}(q) = G(q)/G(\bar{q})$. It follows that mean durationis higher, (i) the less favourable is the term structure of the short-term unemployed, (ii) the higher is the ratio of long-term unemployment to total unemployment, and (iii) the lower is the hazard rate for the long-term unemployed.

The loss of human capital during unemployment can be calculated as the difference between the human capital of the employed and the average human capital of the unemployed. In general, the latter is

$$m_h = \int_0^{\infty} g(q) h(q)\, \mathrm{d}q. \tag{23}$$

The integral can be solved for the short-term unemployed to yield

$$m_h^{st} = \bar{h} + r \int_0^{\bar{q}} G^{st}(q)\, \mathrm{d}q, \tag{24}$$

while the average human capital of the long-term unemployed is $\bar{h}$. Hence eq. (23) can be written:

$$m_h = \bar{h} + rz, \tag{25}$$

where it should be noted that the steady state value of z depends negatively on r. Using eq. (25), the total loss in human capital can be calculated as $(h_0 - \bar{h} - rz)\, U$.

3 The Effect of Deterioration of Human Capital on the Beveridge Curve

In this section the steady-state relationship between unemployment and vacancies, as implied by the given model, will be analysed. To begin with, the case $r = 0$ is chosen for reference purposes. According to our definitions, no long-term unemployment occurs in the special case when unemployment does not affect human capital. Under this condition total unemployment simply is

$$U(k) = \frac{U_0}{1 - e^{-k}}. \tag{26}$$

Eq. (26) implies a stable inverse relationship between vacancies V and unemployment U which is convex to the origin and can be taken as a theoretical foundation of the Beveridge curve [see, for example, Franz (1987)].

If deterioration of human capital during unemployment is introduced ($r > 0$), some of the unemployed loose all their 'perishable' skills. Total unemployment is the sum of short-term and long-term unemployment:

$$\begin{aligned} U(k, r, \sigma) &= U^{st} + U^{lt} \\ &= U_0[s^{st}(k, r, \sigma) + s^{lt}(k, r, \sigma)] \end{aligned}$$

with

$$s^{lt}(k, r, \sigma) \equiv \frac{e^{-L(\bar{q};k,\sigma)}}{1 - e^{-k\sigma}}.$$

and

$$s^{lt}(k, r, \sigma) \equiv \frac{e^{l(\bar{q},k,\sigma)}}{1 - e^{-k\sigma}}.$$

Eq. (27) also defines a steady-state relationship between vacancies and unemployment, but with different characteristics as compared to eq.(26). *Figure 2* shows the results of numerical simulations of eq. (27) for different parameter values r and σ. To transform the results into unemployment and vacancy *rates* an inflow to unemployment of 300000 persons per month and a labour force of 25 millions was assumed, which roughly represents the situation of the German labour market in 1987. In the first simulation the parameter σ was chosen as 0.3, in the second as 0.5 (whereas the former is rather realistic for German data as will be shown below). To obtain a Beveridge-type relationship, the labour market parameter k was varied in the range 0.15 to 2.0 for given r and σ.

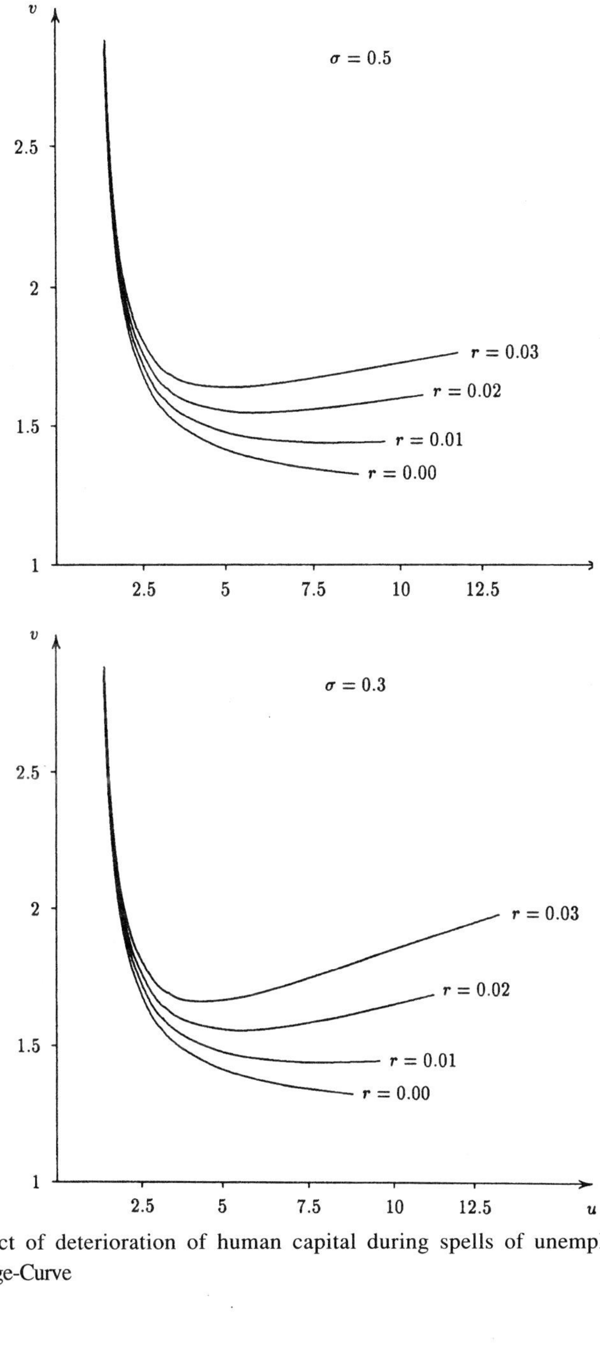

Fig. 2. The effect of deterioration of human capital during spells of unemployment on the Beveridge-Curve

For $r = 0$ the simulation yields the traditional Beveridge curve which neglects the effect of deterioration of human capital during unemployment. It is evident from this figure, that the Beveridge curves for $r > 0$ converge to the standard case in situations of strong excess demand on the labour market. Marked deviations, however, occur in a regime of predominant excess supply on the labour market. Hence, as might be clear from intuition, the effect of deterioration of human capital appears to be primarily a phenomenon of 'bad times'.

As can be seen from *figure 2*, the Beveridge curve will be a declining function if r does not exceed 0.02 and unemployment u is below 5%. In slack labour markets the curve for $r = 0.01$ becomes rather flat, indicating that a wide range of unemployment rates is compatible with almost the same vacancy rate in a steady state situation. For larger values of the deterioration parameter, the simulated steady-state Beveridge curve even has a *positive* slope in the high-unemployment region. The comparison between the lower and upper part of *figure 2* shows that this effect is less striking if the non-perishable part of human capital is larger (as should be expected). But also with σ set to 0.5 the steady-state Beveridge curve is upward sloping in the high unemployment region when r is 0.02 or higher.

These results have some important implications. If the Beveridge curve is almost horizontal or positively sloping within a certain range, combinations of u and v are no longer unique. According to the simulations we may, for example, obtain almost the same vacancy rate in a situation of low (say 4%) and high (say 8%) unemployment rate if the deterioration parameter r is 0.02 and $\sigma = 0.3$. Thus, significant deterioration of human capital during unemployment results in a situation of multiple equilibria. Moreover, if deterioration of human capital takes place very quickly, then in slack labour markets an even higher number of vacancies might be required to prevent unemployment from further rising than in high employment periods.

For an explanation of this result a comparison with the standard matching model is helpful: If spells of unemployment do not affect human capital ($r = 0$), the number of unfilled vacancies falls monotonically when unemployment rises. The reason is that with more persons being unemployed the chance diminishes that an applicant drawn by a specific labour-seeking firm is not available because he has been sucessful elsewhere. As a consequence, the number of vacancies required to keep the unemployment rate constant, falls with a growing excess supply of labour. In the case of a marked deterioration of human capital during unemployment, however, the positive effect of growing unemployment on the matching probability can be over-compensated by a negative effect. This negative effect is caused by the fact that the mean duration of unemployment is higher and human capital of the unemployed in the average is lower when labour markets are slack. Thus, an increasing portion of the unemployed does not meet the reservation productivity of the firms and the matching probability falls. Consequently, the steady-state condition only holds, if the number of vacancies rises. The deterioration of the *u-v-*

trade-off expresses the costs of an unfavourable term structure in the distribution of unemployment when labour markets are characterised by a high excess supply.

Table 1. Inflows and outflows from unemployment and the unemployment rate 1980–1987

year	unemployment level	rate	inflows	outflows
1980	888900	3.8	3084068	2832549
1981	1271574	5.5	3531038	2945478
1982	1833244	7.5	3706655	3187165
1983	2258235	9.1	3704185	3578551
1984	2265559	9.1	3672791	3696594
1985	2304014	9.3	3750240	3728294
1986	2228004	9.0	3637266	3766214
1987	2228788	8.9	3726460	3636411

Notes:– Source: Bundesanstalt für Arbeit, ANBA, 5, 1988

4 A Look at the Data

In order to check whether a flat or even rising steady-state Beveridge curve might be relevant in reality, we concentrate on recent German labour market data. *Table 1* gives some overall indicators of the labour market situation in the eighties. Inflows into unemployment were rising considerably during the OPEC II recession, followed by a rise in outflows from unemployment with a marked lag. Since 1983 inflows and outflows were roughly constant at a level of about 3.7 millions per year, and the overall unemployment rate remained almost constant at a level of about 9%. It is evident that in the latter time period the labour market situation was close to a steady state. If some lags of adjustment are allowed for[4], these data can be used to estimate a steady-state distribution of unemployment.

From the yearly special inquest of the Federal Employment Bureau (Bundesanstalt für Arbeit) in May/June data for completed spells of overall unemployment are available which are divided into those which are completed before 1, 3, 6, 12 and 24 months. From the same source data for extreme long-term unemployment (2 and more years) exist.

In order to apply the theoretical model to the data, the critical duration $\bar{q}$, after which a typical unemployed person has totally lost the perishable part of its human

[4] The observation period was 1984-1987 for this reason.

capital, must be specified. The official definition takes unemployment up to 12 months as 'short-term employment'. To employ this definition in our framework would imply the deterioration process of human capital being completed after one year of unemployment. Inspection of the data, however, suggests that this is not the case. Instead, since hazard rates are less different after unemployment duration of 2 years and longer, the critical duration $\bar{q}$ was chosen as 24 months.[5]

Table 2. Survivor function for unemployment (1984–1987)

year	Survival rates after month				
	1	3	6	12	24
	including discouraged workers				
1984	0.882	0.678	0.432	0.181	0.046
1985	0.865	0.636	0.368	0.158	0.039
1986	0.839	0.599	0.349	0.139	0.044
1987	0.832	0.591	0.332	0.137	0.047
	excluding discouraged workers				
1984	0.859	0.628	0.364	0.128	0.030
1985	0.848	0.597	0.316	0.121	0.027
1986	0.817	0.553	0.291	0.100	0.030
1987	0.803	0.534	0.264	0.089	0.027

Notes: – calculations by the author; source for original data: Bundesanstalt für Arbeit, ANBA, 5, 1988, p. 774.

The unemployment data with duration up to 24 months were used to calculate survivor functions under the steady-state assumption 'inflows = outflows' (*see table 2*). Since the data allow for discrimination between outflows into employment and in non-employment, where the latter essentially captures the discouraged worker effect, *table 2* gives two versions, with and without taking account of the discouraged worker effect.

[5] According to our calculations, hazard rates after one year of unemployment are nearly as twice as high as those after two years of unemployment. For a duration of more than 2 or 3 years, respectively, hazard rates between 0.07 and 0.05 are calculated. Hence, the assumption of constant hazard rates for long-term unemployment with a duration of more than 24 months seems far less critical with respect to the data than applying the same assumption to the official definition. Of course, this deviation from the standard definition implies that the notion 'short-term unemployment' in the theoretical model should not be taken too literally.

Table 3. Non-linear least squares estimation of the survivor function (1984–1987)

coefficient	regression (1)		regression (2)	
	coeff.	s.e.	coeff.	s.e.
$r \times 10^2$	2.562**	0.205	2.937	0.179
k	0.204**	0.011	0.254**	0.013
statistics				
R^2	0.999		0.999	
s.e.	0.078		0.091	

Notes: – ** indicates significance at the 1\% level
– regression (1) : including discouraged worker effect
– regression (2) : excluding discouraged worker effect

Let $s(q)$ be the log of the survivor function $S(q)$. Taking differences between the data for q and $q + n$ and re-arranging gives

$$s(q+n) - s(q) + n = \frac{1}{kr} e^{-k(1-rq)}(e^{krn} - 1), \tag{28}$$

which can be estimated by non-linear least squares techniques.[6] The results are shown in *table 3*. In the first regression the discouraged-worker effect was included in the data, while in the second only those outflows from unemployment were considered which led to new employment contracts. In both regressions r-squared is close to one. The parameters have the expected sign and are significant at the one percent level. The estimated k-coefficient is 0.20 in the first regression and somewhat higher (0.25) in the second. The deterioration parameter r is estimated as being higher (0.029) when the data are corrected for the discouraged worker effect against a value of 0.026 for the uncorrected data. This result reflects the fact that the discouraged worker effect increases markedly with longer duration of unemployment.

The magnitude and the high significance of the deterioration parameter r indicate that hazard rates decline considerably during unemployment. For a person who has just become unemployed the probability of getting a job within the next month is approximately 0.22, after one year of unemployment this probability falls to 0.15

[6] Since 'vacancies' in the sense of our theoretical model are not identical with the statistical concept of this variable, the parameter k as the ratio of vacancies to unemployment cannot be taken directly from labour market data but has to be estimated.

and after two years of unemployment it is about 0.07 only.[7] Given the hazard rates of (extreme) long-term unemployment, estimated values of k of 0.20 to 0.25 yield estimates of the parameter σ of 1/4 to 1/3. As has been shown in the previous section by numerical simulations, the parameter constellation obtained empirically, would imply a (moderately) upward sloping steady-state Beveridge curve in the relevant region.

Conclusion

Deterioration of human capital during periods of unemployment is one channel through which the hysteresis effect might come into effect. Sorting processes as well as duration-caused human capital depreciation may be responsible for this phenomenon. The theoretical model adopted here assumes a linear 'deterioration function' for a representative unemployed person and analyses the consequences for the matching process in a probabilistic model. It can be shown that the steady-state Beveridge curve, which allows for hazard rates of the unemployed to decline with longer duration of unemployment, bends away from the standard u-v-curve in situations of excess supply on the labour markets. This effect implies that the same vacancy rate might be compatible with different unemployment rates, so that a situation of multiple equilibria arises. The larger is the deterioration parameter r and the lower the non-perishable part of human capital, the more likely is the occurrence of multiple equilibria. It can be shown that under specific assumptions about the distribution of reservation productivity of firms that the steady-state distribution of unemployment with respect to unemployment duration can be described by a Gompertz-Makeham distribution. Since the aggregate German labour market came close to a steady state between 1984 to 1987, existing data of completed spells of unemployment for this time period can be used to estimate the parameters of the steady state distribution empirically. It turns out that the deterioration parameter is highly significant and in a order of magnitude which at least does not exclude the possibility of multiple equilibria.

If the vacancy rate is related to wage inflation, we may conclude that a low-inflation economy is possible as well as in a state of low unemployment as in a state of high unemployment. Analysing these effects in more detail would require the integration of the labour market approach adopted here in an broader macroeconomic

[7] This numbers somewhat underestimate the deterioration effect since with longer duration a growing part of the unemployed profits by public job creation ('Arbeitsbeschaffungsmassnahmen') or wage subsidies ('Eingliederungsbeihilfen'). Correcting for this effect, however, only led to minor modifications of the reported results.

model which is beyond the scope of the present paper. The possibility, however, that the economy has settled on a high unemployment equilibrium while a low unemployment equilibrium with the same inflation characteristics exists, has such far-reaching policy implications that it should by itself attract further research.

References

Blanchard O J, Summers L H (1986) Hysteresis and the European unemployment problem, in: S. Fischer (ed.), NBER Macoeconomics Annual (MIT Press, Cambridge): 15–78

Blossfeld H P, Hamerle A, Mayer K U (1989) Event History Analysis – Statistical Theory and Application in the Social Sciences (Lawrence Erlbaum, Hillsdale, N. J.)

Budd A, Levine P, Smith P (1987) Long-term unemployment and the shifting U-V-curve – A multi-country study, European Economic Review 31: 296–305

Budd A, Levine P, Smith P (1988) Unemployment, vacancies and the long-term unemployed, Economic Journal, 98: 1071–1091

Burda M (1988) Is there a capital shortage in Europe? Weltwirtschaftliches Archiv 124: 38–57.

Franz W (1987) Strukturelle und friktionelle Arbeitslosigkeit in der Bundesrepublik Deutschland – Eine theoretische und empirische Analyse der Beveridge Kurve, in: Bombach, G., Gahlen, B., Ott, A. E. (eds.), Arbeitsmärkte und Beschäftigung, Schriftenreihe des wirtschaftswissenschaftlichen Seminars Ottobeuren, Bd. 16, Tübingen 1987

Gottfries N, Horn H (1987) Wage formation and the persistence of unemployment, Economic Journal 97: 877–884

Hargraves Heap S P (1980) Choosing the wrong natural rate: Accelerating inflation or deceleration employment and growth, Economic Journal 90: 611–620

Lindbeck A, Snower D J (1986a) Explanations of unemployment, Oxford Review of Economic Policy 1: 34–59

Lindbeck A, Snower D J (1986b) Wage Setting, Unemployment and Insider-Outsider Relations, American Economic Review 76: 235–239

Lindbeck A, Snower D J (1987a) Union activity, unemployment persistence and wage-employment ratchets, European Economic Review 31: 157–167

Lindbeck A, Snower D J (1987b) Efficiency Wages versus insiders and outsiders, European Economic Review 31: 407–416

Phelps E S (1970) Money wage dynamics and labor market equilibrium, in: Phelps, E. S. (ed.), Microeconomic foundations of employment and inflation theory (Macmillan, London)

Phelps E S (1972) Inflation policy and unemployment theory (Macmillan, London)

Pissarides C (1986) Unemployment and Vacancies in Britain, Economic Policy 3: 499–559

Tötsch I (1988) Screening in labour markets with heterogeneous workers, in: Cross, R. (ed.), Unemployment, hysteresis and the natural rate hypothesis (Basil Blackwell, Oxford): 180–200.

Hysteresis, Nairu and Long Term Unemployment in Austria[1]

By P. Neudorfer[2], K. Pichelmann[2] and M. Wagner[3]

Abstract: The paper analyzes hysteresis or persistence effects in Austrian unemployment using formal unit root tests and a simple macroeconometric model of wage-price formation. The empirical results point towards a considerable amount of persistence in unemployment generated by the rising share of long-term unemployed that has been associated with the increase in overall unemployment in Austria.

1 Introduction

The rising tide of unemployment which has swept over Europe since the mid-1970s has confronted most European economies with steadily upward ratcheting unemployment rates. But while there are plenty of explanations for the initial lift-off phases, the fact that unemployment has remained stubbornly high into the late 1980's has posed a challenge to traditional Keynesian or classical theories of macroeconomic fluctuations. Most mainstream explanations presume that the economy should return to some supply-side determined "natural" rate of unemployment. As an alternative to traditional thinking the hypothesis has been put forward that unemployment may be strongly dependent on its own history, a phenomenon called "hysteresis" (if no long run NAIRU exists at all) or "persistence" (if the short run NAIRU converges rather slowly towards its long run level).

The purpose of this paper is to put the persistence model to a test for Austria. This is done in two ways: Firstly, the test is carried out within a time series framework, with little a priori specification of underlying functional relationships. Se-

[1] We would like to thank A. Jäger, R. Kunst and two referees of this Journal for helpful comments.

[2] Peter Neudorfer, Institute for Advanced Studies A-1060 Vienna, Stumpergasse 56.

[3] Michael Wagner, Institute for Economic and Social Research, A-1140 Vienna, Breitenseer Straße 37/11.

condly, against the background of the results of this analysis, another test is applied, this time within the framework of a mainstream functional model relating unemployment to price dynamics.

2 Time Series Evidence of Persistence

In the discussion of the persistence behaviour of the unemployment rate, econometric evidence of non-stationariness became a popular starting point of the analysis (see e.g. Barro 1988). Strictly speaking – as explosive cases are neglected – the hypothesis of a distinct class of non-stationary models, which include a autoregressive unit root, is tested.

$$\phi(L)\,(1-L)\,Y_t = \phi(L)\,\Delta Y_t = \theta(L)\,e_t. \tag{1}$$

In contrast to a stationary process, model (1) implies that a shock at time t would entail a permanent shift in the level of Y_t. The characteristic that at last some fraction of an innovation is permanent gives rise to the "shock persistence" behaviour of a series with an AR unit root.

Table 1. Tests for autoregressive unit roots
Number of observations = 144

series	k	d^{μ}	d^{τ}	q^{μ}	q^{τ}
LUR	1	–1.522	–0.746	–4.101	–2.456
$\Delta\, LUR$	1	–7.576***	–7.874***	–98.482***	–101.73***

Notes: d^{μ}, d^{τ}, are the Dickey-Fuller test statistics in a model excluding and including a linear trend; q^{μ}, q^{τ} are the respektive Stock-Watson test statistics; *** indicate the rejection of the null hypothesis of a unit root at 1% significance level; k is the number of autoregressive corrections

We first apply two formal unit root tests to the log of the quarterly, seasonally adjusted unemployment rate (LUR) from 1951 to 1986. Both the well-known Dickey-Fuller procedure (1979) and a test provided by Stock and Watson (1986) rest on the assumption that the data generating process has a sufficient AR representation, i.e., they depend on the use of appropriate AR polynomials. To specify the order of lags we considered the values suggested by the (partial) autocorrelation. As an *MA* (1) was strongly supported, we fitted an *AR* (1) approximation.

Table 1 shows the results of the tests applied to the levels and first differences of *LUR*. The null hypothesis of a unit root cannot be rejected regardless of the model, i.e., with or without a trend. For the first differences the test rejects the null hypothesis in all specifications, strongly supporting the hypothesis of an integration of order one. It may be interesting to note that the same qualitative results are obtained for a shorter sample period ending in 1982, thereby excluding the increase in unemployment in the eighties.

However, as Campbell and Mankiw (1987) showed, first order integration alone is not sufficient for assessing the magnitude of shock persistence. Since the amount of long-run persistence also depends on the value of the *MA* coefficients, they suggest *ARMA* modelling for the first differences. Consider the moving average representation of (1)

$$\Delta Y_t = \phi(L)^{-1}\theta(L)\, e_t = A(L)\, e_t. \tag{2}$$

Under the hypothesis that ΔY_t is stationary, $\sum A_i^2$ is finite, implying that the limit of A_i is zero as i approaches infinity. Then an *MA* representation of the level of the process

$$Y_t = (1-L)^{-1}A(L)\, e_t = B(L)\, e_t \tag{3}$$

can be found, where the coefficients of $B(L)$ are given by

$$B_\tau = \sum A_i \qquad\qquad i = 0,\ldots \tau. \tag{4}$$

If Y_t is non-stationary, the limit of B_T (for T approaching infinity) is not zero. It indicates by how much an innovation changes a forecast over a long term horizon. After having determined $A(L)$ on the basis of an adequate *ARMA* model, the values of B_T for large T (i.e. the response of LUR_{T+t} to an innovation at time t) can be calculated easily. The limit of B_T is the infinite sum of A_i coefficients, $A(L = 1)$, which also can be directly computed.

Following the approach of Campbell and Mankiw we estimated several *ARMA* models up to order (3,3) for the first differences of *LUR* using a simple maximum-likelihood procedure. Table 2 shows the respective impulse response models calculated on the basis of the *MA* representation of the first differences according to equation (4).

All specifications lead to the result of a long term persistence *greater than one*. Therefore a 1% innovation in the unemployment rate increases the univariate forecast between 1.3% and 1.9% over any predictable long term horizon. In the short run the results give an even more uniform picture, indicating an impulse response of 1.3% to 1.5%.

Table 2. Model impulse response, *LUR*

model p, q	1	2	3	12	20	40	∞
1,0	1.321	1.424	1.467	1.472	1.472	1.472	1.472
1,1	1.361	1.393	1.396	1.396	1.396	1.396	1.396
1,2	1.359	1.389	1.402	1.410	1.410	1.410	1.410
1,3	1.333	1.367	1.463	1.512	1.513	1.513	1.513
2,0	1.352	1.365	1.330	1.317	1.315	1.317	1.317
2,1	1.360	1.357	1.344	1.344	1.344	1.344	1.344
2,2	1.426	1.431	1.469	1.460	1,456	1.454	1.454
2,3	1.487	1.445	1.535	1.530	1.521	1.521	1.508
3,0	1.371	1.360	1.416	1.508	1.509	1.509	1.509
3,1	1.355	1.346	1.378	1.700	1.739	1.745	1.745
3,2	1.267	1.325	1.451	1.889	1.897	1.895	1.895
3,3	1.301	1.322	1.449	1.766	1.779	1.779	1.779
0,1	1.353	1.353	1.353	1.353	1.353	1.353	1.353
0,2	1.365	1.367	1.387	1.387	1.387	1.387	1.387
0,3	1.440	1.454	1.291	1.291	1.291	1.291	1.291

Notes: B_T, the persistence measure at time T, equals ΣA_t ($t = 0, \ldots T$), where A_t are the *MA* representation $A(L)$ (impulse response function) of the respective *ARIMA* (p, 1, q)-model; the persistence at ∞ is obtained by evaluating this *MA* Lag-polynominal at $A(L = 1)$. According to the *AIC*, the initially proposed (0, 1, 1) *ARIMA* model seems appropriate.

3 Explanations for Persistence

There are several explanations for persistence of unemployment (as defined in our time series test for Austrian data). A first explanation focusses on the role of capital formation.

Persisting unemployment can result if deteriorating demand expectations and adverse movements in profitability lead to a reduction in capital formation which, in turn, may cause a "capital shortage" to emerge. If there are only limited possibilities for short-run variations in the capital-labour mix, the existing capital stock may pose a barrier to higher employment. Thus, under this scenario (proposed in particular by Malinvaud 1982; see also Modigliani et al. 1987), higher investment is a necessary precondition of improved labour market conditions.

A second view is provided by the insider-outsider hypothesis of wage-setting behaviour. If unions bargain mainly on behalf of the incumbent workforce but care less about the welfare of the unemployed "outsiders", then any temporary adverse effect on employment will tend to perpetuate itself as real wage demands are adapted to the now smaller number of employed "insiders" (standard references are Gregory 1986, Blanchard and Summers 1986, and Lindbeck and Snower 1986, 1988).

A third explanation has it that persistence might arise because individual worker skills and work habits deteriorate in a period of prolonged unemployment. Even if the quantitative importance of human capital depreciation is considered to be fairly small, those with a long history of unemployment may become less attractive to prospective employers if these use past unemployment records of the job applicants as a screening device. The resulting disenfranchisement from the labour markets implies that the long-term unemployed exert little or no downward pressure on wage increases. Obviously, this view is closely related to the insider-outsider hypothesis. It simply puts more emphasis on "outsider" mechanisms. According to this view, then, a growing proportion of long-term unemployment should lead to an outward shift of the Beveridge curve as well as to an increase of the NAIRU (see e.g. Layard and Nickell 1986 and Franz 1987, who have argued along these lines).

Before testing the persistence hypothesis within our preferred model of the NAIRU, it might be worthwhile to look at some of the more salient features of unemployment and its relation to price inflation.

4 Features of Austrian Unemployment

Unemployment began to rise in Austria during the early eighties. First the entries into the unemployment register accelerated substantially from about 250 000 (1980) to close to 400 000 persons (1982). Average spell duration hardly changed. From 1983 onwards, it has been rather the lengthening of spells than inflow numbers which has been contributing to the rise in the rate of unemployment (Table 3).

Although the turnover in unemployment is still high compared to that of other European countries which have been experiencing high unemployment for a longer period of time, there are indications that the pool of unemployed has become increasingly segmented.

Empirical evidence from escape rate models for a six year panel of Austrian unemployed suggests that exit probabilities from unemployment are considerably less for the long-term than for the short-term unemployed. Furthermore, for unemployed individuals with previous spells of unemployment the average spell duration becomes longer if the previous spell lasted for more than six months (Frühstück, Pichelmann 1987). From these results one would expect that the rise in the share of long-term unemployed (more than one year) from an average of 8.2% (1974–1982) to 12% (1983–1986) should have been associated with an outward shift of the Austrian Beveridge curve. And indeed, the results of Christl (1987) confirm that about one half of the observable outward shift of the Beveridge curve since 1983 can be attributed to the higher level of long-term unemployment.

Table 3. Austrian unemployment: inflow and outflow patterns

Year	Rate of unemployment (national definition)	Monthly inflow in % of employment	Monthly outflow in % of unemployment
	(Average of monthly values)		
1980	1.88	1.00	59.72
1981	2.42	1.37	57.25
1982	3.67	1.73	46.57
1983	4.45	1.81	41.08
1984	4.54	1.74	38.73
1985	4.81	1.65	33.20
1986	5.18	1.57	29.69
1987	5.58	1.44	26.63

Source: Pichelmann (1987); updated for 1987.

This evidence suggests that the long term unemployed carry little weight in Austrian wage-price formation, which is shaped by corporatist income policies. Their institutional set-up gives indeed very little voice to "outsiders". It is the major powerful organizations of interest mediation which determine the distribution of income between factors of production and households. It has been a critical question for some time whether such macroeconomic actors pay due attention to "outside" minorities. If this were the case, the unemployment rate should be an important variable in explaining wage formation; moreover, the lengthening of unemployment spells should not weaken the impact on wage moderation. Thus our null hypothesis would be that in corporatist Austria wage-price mechanisms are well designed to cope with higher unemployment and the associated rise in the share of long-term unemployment.

5 A *NAIRU*-Framework for Testing for Hysteresis

To test directly for the impact of long-term unemployment on wage-price dynamics in Austria we make use of a macroeconomic framework of wage-price determination described, for example, in Layard and Nickell (1986) and Nickell (1987). The general idea is a "Battle of the Mark-Ups" approach with unemployment serving to reconcile the "feasible" real wage implied by the pricing behaviour of firms and the "target" real wage implied by the wagesetting behaviour of wage-bargainers in the long run.

The wage-price system takes the general form

Price-Setting:

$$p - w = f(w - w^e, x, y, Z_p) \tag{5}$$

Wage-Bargaining:

$$w - p = g(p - p^e, x, U, Z_w) \tag{6}$$

where w denotes hourly labour cost (incl. employers' contributions to social security), p is value-added prices and x denotes productivity; y is designated to describe the level of activity in the output market which may affect the markup behaviour and Z_p stands for possible long-run price pressure variables. Analogously, Z_w denotes wage-pressure elements such as tax rates, mismatch indices or replacement ratios; *U* is designated to capture the influence of labour-market activity on wage-bargaining outcomes. The equilibrium rate of unemployment or the *NAIRU* may then be conveniently defined as the rate of unemployment that reconciles real wage claims and price-mark ups, when – for simplicity – y is set to its average value.

In the empirical implementation of the equation system outlined above we adopt an error-correction framework. The price/wage surprise variables are represented by the changes in price/wage inflation and for the productivity variable we simply employ output per man-hour. Of the many variables we have tried for Z_w, we have only found changes in indirect taxes to be of significant importance. In Table 4 we report a series of six wage equations which differ only with respect to the specification of the unemployment terms. All equations are jointly estimated with a price equation (not reported here; estimates for the price equation corresponding to our finally preferred wage equation are depicted in an Appendix) by an 3SLS/IV-procedure.

Table 4. Aggregate wage equations: Austria 1966–1986

	Dependent Variable: $\Delta(w-p)$					
Independent Variables	(I)	(II)	(III)	(IV)	(V)	(VI)
Constant	–1.699 (4.4)	–1.602 (5.4)	–1.774 (4.8)	–1.744 (5.8)	–1.683 (6.2)	–1.940 (5.6)
$(w-p)_{-1}$	–0.374 (4.3)	–0.348 (5.2)	–0.390 (4.6)	–0.380 (5.6)	–0.366 (5.9)	–0.422 (5.3)
$\Delta^2 p$	–0.848 (6.1)	–0.635 (6.0)	–0.805 (6.0)	–0.832 (6.3)	–0.717 (7.2)	–0.755 (5.6)
x_{-1}	0.419 (3.8)	0.378 (4.4)	0.436 (4.1)	0.411 (4.8)	0.397 (5.0)	0.472 (4.6)
Δtax	–0.881 (4.1)	–1.134 (6.2)	–0.906 (4.2)	–0.984 (4.2)	–0.833 (4.9)	–0.923 (4.9)
Unemployment terms:						
U	–0.02716 (3.5)	–0.00919 (5.4)	–	–	–	–0.01620 (7.6)
U_{-1}	0.01683 (1.9)	–	–	–	–	–
ΔU	–	–0.01338 (2.5)	–	–	–	–
U^S	–	–	–0.02559 (3.3)	–0.01954 (3.8)	–0.01680 (4.8)	–
U^S_{-1}	–	–	0.01236 (1.4)	–0.00020 (0.0)	–	–
U^L	–	–	–	0.04099 (1.0)	–0.01582 (0.4)	–
U^L_{-1}	–	–	–	–	0.05188 (1.6)	–
(U^L/U)	–	–	–	–	–	0.00287 (2.8)
$S.E.$	0.01089	0.00825	0.01046	0.00872	0.00894	0.01023
DW	2.28	2.29	2.24	2.22	2.47	2.04

3SLS/IV – Estimation

We will not separately discuss the variables other than the labour market activity variables since, generally speaking, they tell the same story in all of the estimated wage equations. The coefficients of lagged real product wages and productivity are consistently of the same order of magnitude. Thus, with respect to the distribution of functional income, there seems to be an error correction mechanism at work which comes close to many descriptive accounts of Austrian collective bargaining. The short-run elasticity of wages with respect to prices lies in the range of .15 to .36.

For our purposes, however, the performance of the various unemployment terms is of crucial importance. Since various attempts with non-linear specifications of the unemployment terms have not proven very sucessful, the first two equations test for the linear effects of the overall unemployment rate. From columns (I) and (II) it becomes evident that both a level and a change term of u are of significant influence. Under the error correction specification the size of the unemployment coefficients implies that an increase in unemployment induces an immediate reduction in real wage growth and thus results in a lower level of real wages in the long-run. Persistent unemployment, however, ceases to affect real wage claims.

The models (III)–(VI) then examine the hypothesis that this result can be atributed to duration composition effects of unemployment. Model (III) differs from (I) in the respect that the overall unemployment rate is replaced by the short-term unemployment rate U^S. While the estimate for the contemporaneous unemployment term hardly changes, it turns out that lagged short-term unemployment is of no importance. It is long-term unemployment that accounts for persistence effects in unemployment; this is the main message from models (IV)–(VI), which illustrate that the long-term unemployed fail to exercise significant influence in wage-bargaining. Thus, a higher share of long-term unemployed in overall unemployment (U^L/U) tends to dampen the restraining impact of unemployment on real wage demands.

Certainly, the share of long-term unemployment in total unemployment is closely related to the level of unemployment itself. This can be illustrated by the following simple regression:

$$U^L/U = \underset{(5.5)}{0.81}\,[U^L/U]_{-1} - \underset{(3.5)}{2.59}\,U + \underset{(4.5)}{6.36}\,U_{-1} - \underset{(2.5)}{3.05}\,U_{-2} \qquad (7)$$

OLS-estimation 1966–1986 $SE = 1.13\%$ $R^2C = 0.74$

These results seem quite plausible. In the short-run the share of long-term unemployment tends to fall with increasing unemployment, because the duration composition is initially driven by increases in the inflow into unemployment. With the elapse of time, however, sorting and selection mechanisms within the unemployment pool (Budd et al. 1986) result in a higher proportion of long-term unemployment when unemployment rises.

Removing the lagged dependent variable and rearranging terms reveals that an unemployment rate of, say, 10% is estimated to be associated with a long-term proportion of about 21%.

$$\frac{U^L}{U} = 2.07\,U - 5.06\,\Delta U + 0.40\,\Delta^2 U + \text{small terms} \tag{8}$$

It may be interesting to note that for any given level of unemployment the implied long-term proportion seems to be lower in Austria than in countries like the Federal Republic of Germany or Britain (compare the results of Franz 1987, and Nickell 1987).

Substituting (8) into model (VI) gives rise to just the kind of dynamics reported in model (II), where overall unemployment is the only relevant labour market activity variable. Thus we are inclined to suggest that the time-dependency of the Austrian *NAIRU* is caused by the duration composition effects of unemployment.

Combining our preferred wage equation (models (II) and (VI), respectively) with the corresponding price equations (see appendix) yields *NAIRU*-estimates for Austria. Despite being still very low by international standards in absolute levels, they indicate the serious impediment to the workings of the labour market that long-term unemployment may pose even in a low-unemployment country like Austria. According to our analysis, some 60% of the one percentage point increase in the contemporaneous *NAIRU* since 1980 to about 4% in 1986 can be attributed to the rise in the long term proportion of the unemployed.

6 Concluding Remarks

This paper has presented some empirical evidence on persistence effects in Austrian unemployment. Using formal time series analysis, it is difficult to reject the hypothesis that there is a random walk component in the unemployment rate. It is well known, however, that the unit root tests have low power against borderline stationary alternatives. An assessment of the magnitude of shock persistence (along the lines of Campell and Mankiw, 1987) has led to the result of a long-term persistence greater than one. This casts some further doubts on the appropriateness of univariate modelling of the unemployment process (for a detailed discussion see Neudorfer and Pichelmann, 1988). Moreover, as Jäger and Kunst (1988) have shown, seasonal adjustment by the Census *X*-11 procedure may lead to an upward bias in these measures of the degree of shock persistence.

We have, therefore, proceeded to test directly for the impact of duration-composition effects of unemployment on wage bargaining in Austria. Employing a simple macroeconomic modell of wage-price formation we have found that the long-term unemployed fail to exercise a restraining impact on real wage demands. The estimates point towares a considerable amount of persistence generated via this channel but not to hysteresis, i.e. there is still a long-run *NAIRU* determined by the underlying working properties of the economy.

The rise in the long-term proportion that has been associated with the increase in overall unemployment since 1981 has thus significantly contributed to the upward shift in the Austrian-*NAIRU*, pushing its contemporaneous value above the corresponding long-run level. This result is consistent with those reported for several other countries (Coe, 1988), It illustrates nicely that persistence effects in unemployment may – as in the Austrian case – show up already after a relatively short period of rising unemployment.

While we have been able to establish that the long-term unemployed tend to become outsiders in the Austrian wage formation process, our analysis falls short of identifying whether it is reduced search intensity of the long-term unemployed or employers' screening mechanisms (or both) that account for the persistence result. More microeconomic evidence – using, in particular, longitudinal data on individual unemployment experience – will have to come forth before firm policy conclusions can be drawn.

Appendix

Aggregate price equations corresponding to models (II) and (VI) in Table 4: Austria 1966–1986

Independent variables:	Depndent variable: $\Delta(p-w)$	
	(II)	(VI)
Constant	1.698	1.642
	(6.0)	(6.0)
$(p-w)_{-1}$	0.343	–0.330
	(5.5)	(5.4)
$\Delta^2 w$	–0.524	–0.511
	(6.8)	(7.0)
x_{-1}	–0.325	–0.310
	(4.1)	(4.0)
*OMA*1	1.321	1.309
	(7.1)	(7.2)
*OMA*2	–0.045	–0.035
	(3.7)	(7.2)
S.E.	0.00909	0.00910
DW	1.74	1.61

3SLS/IV-Estimation

Notes: p, w and x are defined in the text; *OMA*1 and *OMA*2 denote variables intended to capture the effects of output market activity on markup behaviour. *OMA*1 is (the log of) overtime hours and *OMA*2 is the (lagged) change in the degree of capacity utilization.

References

Barro R J (1988) The persistence of unemployment. American Economic Review PAP 78/2: 32–37

Blanchard O J, Summers L H (1986) Hysteresis and the European unemployment problem. NBER Macroeconomics Annual 1986, MIT Press, Cambridge: 15–78

Budd A, Levine P, Smith P (1986) Real wage adjustment and longterm unemployment. Discussion Paper No. CEF 21–86, London Business School

Campbell J Y, Mankiw N G (1987) Are output fluctuations transitory? Quarterly Journal of Economics 102: 857–880

Christl J (1987) Steigt die strukturelle Arbeitslosigkeit? In: BM für Arbeit und Soziales (ed) Die Dynamik des Arbeitsmarktes, Forschungsberichte aus Sozial- und Arbeitsmarktpolitik 19, Wien

Coe D T (1988) Hysteresis Effects in Aggregate Wage Equations. In: R Cross (ed) Unemployment, hysteresis & the natural rate hypothesis, Basil Blackwell

Dickey D A, Fuller WA (1979) Distribution of the estimator for autoregressive time series with a unit root. Journal of the American Statistical Association 74: 427–431.

Franz W (1987) Hysteresis, persistence, and the NAIRU: An empirical analysis for the Federal Republic of Germany. In: R Layard, L Calmfors (ed) The Fight Against Unemployment, Centre for European Policy Studies, MIT-Press

Frühstück E, Pichelmann K (1987) Abgangsraten aus dem Leistungsbezug bei Arbeitslosigkeit. Research Memorandum, Institute for Advanced Studies, Vienna

Gregory R (1986) Wage policy and unemployment in Australia. Economica 53 (Supplement): 53–74

Jäger A, Kunst R (1988) Seasonal adjustment and measuring persistence in output. Institute for Advanced Studies Vienna, Research Memorandum No. 247.

Layard R, Nickell S (1986) Unemployment in Britain, Economica 53 (Supplement): 121–169

Lindbeck A, Snower D J (1986) Wage setting, unemployment and insider-outsider relations. American Economic Review 76/2: 235–239

Lindbeck A, Snower D J (1988) Long-term unemployment and macroeconomic policy. American Economic Review 78/2: 38–43

Malinvaud E (1982) Wages and unemployment. Economic Journal 92: 1–12

Modigliano F, Monti M, Drèze J H, Giersch H, Layard R (1987) Reducing Unemployment in Europe: The Role of Capital Formation. In: R Layard, L Calmfors (ed) The fight against unemployment, Centre for European Policy Studies, MIT-Press

Neudorfer P, Pichelmann K (1988) Measuring shock persistence in Austrian employment and unemployment series. Research Memorandum No. 252, Institute for Advanced Studies, Vienna

Nickell S (1987) Why is wage inflation in Britain so high? Oxford Bulletin of Economics and Statistics 49/1: 103–128

Pichelmann K (1987) Konzentration und Dauer von Arbeitslosigkeit in Österreich. In: KW Rothschild, G Tichy (ed) Arbeitslosigkeit und Arbeitsangebot in Österreich, Springer-Verlag

Stock J H, Watson M W (1986) Testing for common trends. Discussion Paper No. 1222, Harvard University